40.

A Visi

Ann Fox

Ann Fox
Rena
23 Sanctuary Rd
Hazlemere
High Wycombe

HAB.2: 1—4

New Wine Press

© 1989 Ann Fox

New Wine Press
P.O. Box 17
Chichester   PO20 6RY
England

ISBN 0 947852 51 4

Dedicated To

The people of West Wycombe, who deserve an explanation.

Acknowledgements

I would like to thank all those who have made this book possible, especially those whose names are mentioned herein.

Thanks are also due to:

— The Thursday Fellowship and others who have supported me with prayer at key moments.

— Dee Cameron and Hilary Taylor who typed the manuscript for me.

— My husband, for his support, and help in proof-reading.

— To John Olhausen, my present Vicar, who has encouraged me to publish and supports the message.

West Wycombe Village

Key

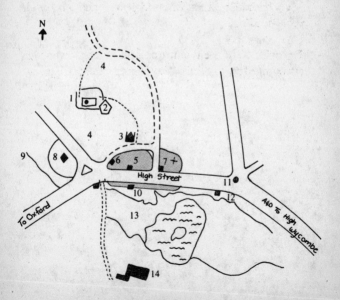

Contents

Chapter 1
The Vision

January 1983

'Where shall I begin to tell the story of how great a love can be?' The famous words of the song 'Love Story' take on a new depth of meaning as I contemplate the eternal love which existed from the beginning, and will never end. I can only attempt to convey that part of God's love which I have experienced personally in recent years. The boundless nature of this love is impossible for us to fully comprehend, but we *can* respond with joy when even a single ray shines into our lives like a shaft of light.

As I begin to write, I feel an excitement, for the Lord himself has urged me to put pen to paper. He has reminded me of a promise I once made, to write a book to the glory of God; the purpose — to illustrate the unravelling of his perfect plan in the lives of ordinary people,

> *'to understand how broad and long, how high and deep is Christ's love.'* (Ephesians 3:18 GNB)

I do not yet know how the story will end, but I write in faith, trusting that this is 'His story' and that even now the Lord is authorising what is yet to happen.

I write carrying a burden and a vision, not on my own behalf, but as a member of the community of West Wycombe. Our burden is a heavy one. A dear friend, once the robust life and soul of the village, now shrinks daily before our eyes, her body racked with bone-cancer. Fearfully we watch her fade, and try to pray, and try to be jolly.

We say, 'Lord, how shall we pray? What can we do to help Diana?' Last week the Lord led me to read Psalm 116. I had pleaded for a word of guidance, to help me in my prayers during this difficult time. Now, here it was in verses 12-14:

> *'What can I offer the Lord for all his goodness to me? I will bring a wine-offering to the Lord, to thank him for saving me. In the assembly of all his people, I will give him what I have promised'.*

(Psalm 116:12-14)

'I will give him what I have promised!' What had I promised? I could think of nothing at first, but a day or two later, whilst relaxing in front of the television, with only half my concentration on the programme, I caught one sentence from the monotonous commentator. The words resounded somewhere between my heart and my head. What had she said?

'Some people write books.'

That was all. And yet I knew it was the answer to my question. Two years earlier, I *had* promised to write a book, to set down all that had happened, before I forgot, because the Lord had given me a vision — a vision for West Wycombe: a great golden cross set on top of West Wycombe Hill, shining with radiant light like a beacon, as a symbol of God's claiming the village for himself, bringing, through his powerful presence, new life to his people.

How would my fulfilling a promise help Diana? Surely it is because Diana has that vision too. So the burden and the vision are bound together by a promise. That is what I must do, for new life, for Diana and for the village, the physical and the spiritual inseparable.

This, then, is my 'wine-offering', my 'sacrifice of thanksgiving'. (Psalm 116:17) May it become the 'cup of salvation' (v.13 KJ) that God requires.

* * * * *

December 1973

I first began to pray for West Wycombe whilst living in Singapore. My husband's work had taken us to the Far East in December 1973. I had great misgivings about the venture. Little did I know then that it would change my life so much. I should have been glad at the chance to opt out of the tedious weekly routine: the full-time teaching, the daily walk home, collecting toddlers from the baby-minder on the way, feeding the family and just managing to do enough housework in between to survive, was not exactly the pleasure it ought to have been. How ungrateful of me to burst into tears when Bruce broke the news. 'We're off to Singapore for six months!' Eight weeks was not long enough to adjust to the idea, for that's all the time we had to pack up, let our house, and say goodbye, before arriving in a strange land seven thousand miles away.

I shall never forget the shock of the heat and humidity as we emerged from the aeroplane, as though stepping from a wintry street through the curtain of hot air at the door of a huge departmental store, only to find one has entered a Turkish Bath. We struggled across the tarmac, feeling clammy and weighed down by our hand-luggage, which we set down as soon as we could in order to peel off layers of redundant clothing — cardigans, anoraks, ties...Too bad about my tights — they would have to stay on! This initial, physical shock was to stay with me and become more intense as time went by, but at that moment I was in too much of a whirl to realise, or even suspect, what the future would hold.

We were whisked away in a bone-shaking taxi to the Hotel Negara where we were to spend Christmas, whilst looking for a house to live in. Once inside the ultra-modern building, I was glad of my tights, since the air-conditioning caused me to shiver. It was sheer bliss, though, to be in drier air and we soon felt comfortable again. The children, Russell and Mark, took a great deal of convincing that they did not need to put on their anoraks before going out for an evening stroll to see the city lights.

The excitement of Christmas was soon over and a furnished house was found for us. The novelty of our new surroundings was already wearing off, and the realities of actually living in a tropical country in the orient were beginning to dawn on me. Our bungalow was small and dark and had no 'front-door', as we understand that expression. The living-room had no windows, but some light and air was allowed to enter by a huge folding door which doubled as the wall at one end of the house. This was usually kept wide open, though, in the hope of a little privacy, we would draw across the huge lockable grille-gates, which made it seem like a prison. The house was surrounded by a storm-gully into which we soon learned not to fall but unfortunately lost many pieces of lego on wet days, as they were washed away into the drains.

It was essential that I have an 'amah' to do the housework for me, since the heat was so exhausting and enervating. Even to make the beds was like hard labour, requiring half an hour recovery period. It was irritating to me to have to watch someone working around me, whilst I languished on the sofa with my embroidery. Suddenly, all that leisure time, that I had previously longed for, lost its appeal, and I found myself restless, edgy, critical of the amah and guilt-ridden about being lazy.

As time went by, I made a few friends and ventured out more often, but new problems set in as I was exposed to the 'Culture Shock' in increasing intensity. Worries turned into fears. I became afraid of riding in buses and taxis because of the high accident rate. All drivers seemed to career down the streets like lunatics, and whereas in Britain we usually have a choice of one or two lanes to drive along, in Singapore there are four, most roads being dual-carriageway. The

4

vehicles would pass so close, that I often thought the driver alongside us would soon be sharing my passenger seat.

Once safely inside a shopping centre, there was still no respite from threatening experiences, as I feared being locked in the lift, and even had to screw up my courage to step on to the escalator — imagining that I would forever miss the first step. There was no peace of mind if I stayed at home either, since the huge ceiling-fan in the middle of the living-room was just on the verge of flying off its bearings, destined to be flung by centrifugal force like a crazy space-ship, slicing with its heavy 'choppers' at everything in its path — or so I thought!

I felt surrounded at all times by unfamiliar and alien faces, sometimes imagining them to be menacing, some-times mocking. Didn't the little old vegetable hawker come ringing her bell at my gate simply to expose my ignorance of kang-kong, lotus-roots, chye-sim, and other weird species? Surely the sullen 'kabun' (gardener) who came weekly to mow my broad-leaved lawn, came in fact to spy through my windows and ogle at my Western ways.

The one friendly foreign face belonged to the grocer who called daily at the house for my order, and seemed to be able to deliver, within a couple of hours, anything I fancied — milk, potatoes, cornflakes, even strawberries — from the Cold Storage Supermarket in the city. Of course, I had to sieve the flour and rice for weevils, but that was the least of my worries.

Far worse, though, than strange faces, was the wild life that abounded. I hated the cockroaches which appeared at every corner of the house, having entered through the plug-holes and open drains in the bathroom and kitchen, and made their way to a convenient drawer to lay their egg-cases. I learnt to classify the omnipresent ants, according to their habit:

the small scatty black;
the small scatty red;
the large red that swarmed over our guava tree

continuously and sewed the leaves together;

the soldier ants which marched in files through the house to salvage even the smallest crumb on the kitchen work-top;

those that lurked in the grass waiting to crawl up your leg when you sat on a bench to eat an ice-cream.

Most kinds would bite ferociously, but not dangerously, like the four-inch centipedes. I also lived in fear of snakes, after two baby ones were swept up from under Russell's bed, and of rats after a nightmare experience of having one run over my bed whilst I was lying in it! I did learn to accept the geckoes which lived on the walls, probably because they ate the detested mosquitoes.

During the first few months, I lived with the hope of soon returning to England, but as time went by, I realised that this was not to be. I learned, with a sinking feeling in my heart, that my husband's office had plenty of work in Singapore, enough to keep Bruce busy for at least another year. I do not remember praying much at first, for although I was a Christian (that is, I firmly believed in God, and how he had sent his son Jesus to die for the sins of the world), I had no special child-to-father relationship with him, and prayer was not so much a joy as a duty. Unfortunately my faith was not vital enough to withstand overwhelming difficulties.

As all hope of a speedy return to England evaporated, I began to experience feelings of panic. At such times, I would desperately appeal to God to 'do something!' But where was he?

1. Indian carrying large kavadi and also walking on burning coals, carrying a baby.

2. Indian with skewers through his face.

Everywhere, in Singapore, there was evidence of religious activity. At the kerbside, Chinese villagers would burn specially printed 'Hell's Bank Notes', believing that the money would be wafted by the smoke into the after-life, to provide comforts for their revered ancestor-spirits.

Five times a day, a call to prayer would be broadcast from towering minarets, reminding faithful Muslims of their ritualistic duties, whilst a keen amateur photographer might easily 'snap' a Hindu undergoing the penance of Kavadi. This involves short spears and hooks being stuck into one's flesh, especially through the tongue and cheeks, whilst in a trance-like state, and walking a pilgrimage thus, carrying the heavy weight of a frame decorated with flowers, fruit and peacock feathers.

The many temples are a great tourist attraction. Some, like the Temple of a Thousand Lights, house relics of Buddha and invite you to try the wheel of fortune, or purchase a lucky straw. Others, such as Tian Hock Keng, are quiet havens where monks in saffron robes worshipfully offer great feasts of colourful food to the spirits whose plaques of remembrance are mounted in glass cases.

I was surrounded by people who were aware of the supernatural life, and questing after a God-like Spirit. I knew that they all lacked the truth, but where was *my* God? I never questioned his existence; I knew he was there, somewhere, but he seemed so far away. 'God's in his heaven, all's right with the world' — except for *my* bit of the world!

I felt a terrible sense of loneliness, not only in a spiritual sense, but in the human sense too. I seemed to be the only one who was unhappy. My neighbours, some local, some expatriates, had all settled into a comfortable way of life and had nothing to complain about. The greatest grumble would be, 'My amah's left me!' I suspected that nobody understood how I felt, no matter how pleasant they may be. Neither could Bruce understand my attitude. He was so enjoying the new scope and responsibility at work in an air-conditioned luxury office that to him life was new and exciting.

I felt utterly isolated. 'Oh God, please help me!' I would shout in my mind. It felt as though God was upstairs in a padded room, where my hammering on the ceiling could make no impression on his ears. If I had ceased my metaphorical battering, I might have heard his quiet tapping in reply, but my prayers were too noisy, and I was not listening for his reply anyway, at least not the still small voice. Perhaps I expected miraculous happenings — divine intervention in the circumstances of my life. Well, a miracle did occur, but not in the way I expected it.

* * * * *

The Lord was already working out his plan for me, although I did not realise it. After we had been in Singapore for about seven or eight months, I made the acquaintance of a Christian lady. It was obvious to me that Judy had something about her that was different from the other friends I had made. She had a calm assurance and a caring nature, so that I felt encouraged to confide in her a little. Although our conversations were mainly about the everyday difficulties of bringing up small children, she must have sensed my deeper, unspoken needs. When, after lending me a few Christian books on child-discipline, she casually invited me to a ladies' meeting at St. George's Episcopalian Church for expatriates, I accepted. The Ex-Bishop of Pakistan, Chandu Rae, was to be the speaker and my interest was aroused.

When I saw him, I was spell-bound. To me, his face shone like that of an angel. A little, wizened, old man, his obvious joy completely captivated me. I listened entranced as he traced his life-story through Hinduism and Buddhism, till he finally found the truth in Christianity. Obviously The Truth had filled him until the Light of it radiated from him. It must have been the same power that attracted the first disciples to Jesus.

After that, I suggested to Bruce that we might go to the church on Sundays, and he made no objection. We began to attend regularly and made new friends there. Bruce had been brought up as a Methodist, until as a teenager he broke away from its tethers. It had not been anything as dramatic as a rejection of God, rather, a lack of attraction to the church.

From time to time, he had been happy to accompany me to a service, but whilst our children were babies, we did not feel welcomed in the formal atmosphere of a church, so our visits were infrequent. Now at last, the Lord had brought us back to the habit of regular worship, and although we were only 'luke-warm' Christians, it was all part of God's plan for us. Let us not criticize 'fringe Christians', for God has certainly led them thus far, and has further plans for them, as long as they will allow him to work in their lives.

* * * * *

Our second Christmas in Singapore was far merrier than the first, with plenty of socialising amongst our new circle of friends. I even cooked a turkey and a Christmas pudding, and we made believe that all was well, and that it was just like being 'at home'. Of course, the frivolity was all on the surface, but deep down inside me, simmering away, depression and fears were steadily gaining momentum.

Another bone of contention was money — or the lack of it. Although Bruce was earning far more than he would in England, it seemed that we were always hard-up, and certainly we always felt like the poor relations beside American and European friends who spent lazy days at the 'Club' swimming pool, whilst several full-time servants held the fort at home. Hanging over our heads was the burden of a two thousand dollar bill for income tax, due very soon. How on earth would we pay it?

10

The fact that we were now church-goers did not help the inner conflict; in fact, it had little relation to my inner-life at all. I enjoyed the hymns, but derived little from the sermon. I consented to reading the 'Confession', but secretly thought that it was a mere formality: of course, I had done nothing wrong — what was there to confess? — Wasn't it *I* who was hard-done by? — Wasn't *I* the long-suffering one being forced to put up with this dreadful foreign country, for at least a year longer than I had expected?

After a 'friend' told me that Chinese robbers are the cleverest in the world, a new fear was added to my list, and news of Western women being raped by the locals was the final straw. The following months were like a very black nightmare. I was leading a double-life — one for show, and one for real at home. Everything was horrid or miserable. I longed to go home to England where life was normal, but the last thing I could do would be to drag Bruce away from the great exciting adventure he was having. The fear of causing him to hate me was the worst fear of all.

He caught me in an hysterical moment, reaching for the alcohol, in order to blot out the thoughts pounding in my brain. I did not even feel ashamed. It was as if I was already drunk with depression. I was convinced that I would never return to England alive, so I might as well end it all here and now by my own hand. I would lie awake at night, tense and scared, turning over the problems in my mind, until I fell asleep through exhaustion, only to cry out in alarm an hour or so later when a subconscious fear overcame me. I would finally give in to sleep with my face buried in the pillow as a safeguard against falling geckoes.

Chapter 2
New Birth

June 1975

I remember sitting by the beautiful MacRitchie Reservoir one afternoon in absolute depression. I could not find in my soul one happy thought. By now, on this blackest of black occasions, I had decided that I was quite incapable of helping myself out of this situation. I came to the conclusion that I must find someone who could help me, someone in authority who would know what to do.

As I sat absent-mindedly staring across the water to the secondary jungle on the far side, an unexpected answer came to me: I must go and see the vicar. Consciously, I thought, 'The Vicar?!' I was somewhat sceptical. 'That rather intellectual individual who loves to preach a social gospel — I don't even know him!' He certainly had not made any impression on me as being deeply spiritual, or even well-qualified as a counsellor, but there seemed to be no other way. He was the only hope on the horizon, albeit a bleak one, and I knew I must try it. When a frantic man is drowning, he clutches at straws.

It was not until the next morning that I had a moment alone to grasp for the telephone.

'Hello, Mr. —, I'd like to make an appointment to see you.'

'Oh, er, all right. How about Wednesday morning in the church office?' came the reply.

'Well, I'll have my little boy, Mark, with me. Will that matter?'

'Oh no', he said, 'he can play on the carpet while we talk'.

And so it was arranged, on Mark's fourth birthday, June 18th, 1975. I shall never forget it. We had been in Singapore for eighteen months, and here I was, telling a vicar, in whom I had scant confidence, that I was desperate with fear and depression, that we had hardly enough money to live on, and that I had no way of coping with the situation. The Reverend was most surprised.

'You never look depressed to me,' he countered, 'I would never have guessed…'.

'Ah,' I assured him, 'I have learned to be a good actress, but all is not as it seems.'

He sought to calm my fears. I hardly understood what he was talking about. He seemed to be referring me to the Greeks, with their gods and goddesses. I do not remember any of his words, but I do recall God's words that he gave me from Philippians 4: 6&7 GNB:

> *'Don't worry about anything, but in all your prayers ask God for what you need, always asking him with a thankful heart. And God's peace, which is far beyond human understanding, will keep your hearts and minds safe in union with Christ Jesus.'*

I have often re-read those verses since that day, and praised the Lord for His words, which are far more powerful than the wise words of men, and for the obedient servant who passed them on.

However, on hearing them for the first time, I cast them aside, feeling they were too simplistic to be useful in my case. Being aware that the vicar was going to pray, I dutifully bowed my head. I felt slightly awkward, but realised that vicars do this sort of thing. I do not remember what he prayed. The words held no significance for me, rang no bells. I was unaware of the power they released; I heard them — that is all.

When it was over, I rose to leave, shook hands and politely thanked the clergyman for his time, privately wondering whether the meeting had been worthwhile. Mark and I took advantage of the shade for a little longer as we walked back through the open-sided aisle of the tropical-style, ex-army church. The hot sun streamed in through the brick arches and the rasping of the cicadas in the surrounding bushes deafened our ears.

Open-sided church of St. George, Singapore.

As we strode down the hill, the sun beating on my head seemed a little kinder, no longer oppressive, and I began to realise a strange new feeling *inside* me too. In place of tension there was a new peace. A real burden on my shoulders had been melted away. The feeling of levity was so physical that my feet hardly touched the ground. I can still remember the sensation of flying down that hill, not with regard to speed, but in freedom of spirit, as if bodily lifted up and bouyant.

The inner peace was giving way to joy as I experienced a great revelation of God's love for me. I was suddenly aware that he was really near me — I was no longer far away from him; I had come into God's presence. He had taken me into His arms and reassured me personally. I knew, really knew, that He loved me so much that nothing else mattered in the whole world. I knew that because He loved me, He cared what happened to me. I was convinced that no matter how many snakes or cockroaches, no matter how many road accidents, burglars or rapists, no matter what disaster might be lurking around the corner, still God was loving me and protecting me. It was a most tremendous healing of my mind. I know it is true that *'Perfect love casts out all fear,'* (1 John 4:18) because God's perfect love cast out *my* fear.

As I continued to 'fly' down that road, the Lord continued to speak to me. His message was penetrating even deeper. I began to reason, 'Even if a snake were to bite me, even if I were to become ill from it, I would have no need to fear since God loves me so much. *Even* if I were to die...'. The ultimate taunt of the devil held no more horror for me.

'Where, Oh death, is your sting?'
(1 Corinthians 15:55 NIV)

Why, that would be the best of all because I would be with my loving God for ever. And if that was God's will, surely He would look after my husband and children. The last ounce of fear had been dealt with.

Suddenly, in front of us, loomed the main road and I was jolted into action. 'Come on Mark', I said, 'Let's go for a walk in the park before we go home.' Even the road seemed easier to cross than usual. As we turned in through the gates of the Botanical Gardens, the magnificent cannas, with their showy red and yellow blooms, greeted us royally. Festoons of bougainvilleas along our way displayed such variety of hues in pinks and reds that I had never noticed before. Mark ran on through those curious Banyan trees that have their huge root-curtains hanging from their branches, and on reaching the marsh-garden, we tip-toed between the pools on narrow flag-stones, admiring the brilliance of the damsel-flies in red, green and turquoise. On we went to the big lake to delight in the antics of the ducks and swans. I do not remember how long we spent in the park, but I do remember a heightened awareness of God's love for His creation, in the colours and shapes He had chosen, which seemed to consolidate the assurance that He had chosen and created me, and all for His pleasure.

*****

Arriving back to the familiar dreary dinginess of our house, I was tempted to wonder how long this new peace would last. My experience had been so special and bewildering that I was not able to talk, even to Bruce, about it. I knew that my depression was healed, but I did not know whether it would return. I decided to wait and see for a while. My trust in God was still very immature. I thought that maybe if I told Bruce that I was healed, it might 'break the spell' and then, perhaps, I would lapse again. I did not want to be laughed at, or even pitied, for my weakness. I hasten to add that this did not amount to a new fear, but was more of a safe-guard!

But I *was* different. When God's love came into my life in such force, it gave me a capacity to love others. Even my amah seemed much more human now! The following Sunday, we went to Church as usual, and after the service we spread out on to the grass to partake of coffee and biscuits, as was the custom. As I greeted my friends, I was acutely aware of a change in my attitude, as though I was on the outside of my body, watching myself. I could see that I had a new confidence. I was no longer a timid, self-conscious, poor relation. I was a special creation of God, just as all these other people were, and we were all equal in His sight. 'Hello Jean, lovely to see you!' I said, and really meant it.

As I encountered first one, and then another of my acquaintances, sipping coffee, making light conversation, it mattered not what they thought of me. Why should it? After all, knowing how much my Heavenly Father loved me had made everything else fade into the background. With God having his rightful significance in my life, all else had been put into its proper perspective.

'But if we live in the light — just as he is in the light — then we have fellowship with one another'
(1 John 1:7 GNB)

I had always been a shy person, finding it difficult to make easy conversation, or to make the first advances towards friendships, although my reserve had often been masked by an independence of thought and a compulsion to stand up for my rights, and what I believed to be right.

I realise now, that I was literally self-conscious, too pre-occupied with wondering what others thought of me, fearful that the impression I was making was not favourable. I felt a need to be accepted and approved of by others, which had the effect of hindering the formation of those very relationships I sought after.

In one lesson, God had given me the power to love others and not expect to receive anything in return. I have never again *needed* to be shy, although from time to time I am reminded that shyness is in my 'old' nature. I am not bound to give in to it now, since God has shown me the way to overcome it.

'If the Son sets you free, you will be free indeed!'
(John 8:36 NIV)

At that time, I had never heard of the phrase 'to be born

again'. I had no idea that Jesus had made this a requirement for entry into the Kingdom of God (John 3:5). I had of course received the traditional and symbolic washing in baptismal water as a baby, but had I really been born again at that time? I had indeed confirmed my vows as a young teenager, because I was considered to be 'the right age' and 'involved with the church'. I was attributed the latter label because I attended services regularly and joined in all the associated activities such as the drama club, and the youth guild. I am not sure what was uppermost in my mind in those days — to know God better, or to make the acquaintance of one or two of the more handsome boys in the congregation!

I remember, as a thirteen year old, my Confirmation was quite an awe-inspiring occasion, particularly when a rather ancient bishop laid his hands on my head. Looking back, however, I see no *evidence* of being born again, or of becoming a new person in Christ, on that day; but rather, a taking of a decision to continue with the course I had chosen in my quest for God. Some men search for God all their days, but do not reach Him because they ignore the sign-post that says *'I am the Way'* (John 14:6).

What I did not fully realise, at that ceremony, was the full meaning and significance of repentance, as the liturgy states:-

'I turn to Christ.

I repent of my sins.

I renounce evil.'

Repentance involves not only the baptismal washing and cleansing from sin, inherited and accumulated, but also a change of direction from self-centred to God-centred. Perhaps seeds were sown by the bishop, but were not allowed to flourish immediately because the thorns of the world grew up and stifled them. However, it makes no difference what we learn with our heads, if we do not really know it in our hearts. When it comes to things of the Spirit, we must know and experience God's lessons in our spirit. We must ask Him to make it real.

Now, by God's grace, in a strange land on the other side of the world, God had done it for me. He had made me a new person through his revelation of love. He had made me a new baby, just setting out on a new kind of Christian life — the real kind, not head but heart. I had a great deal to learn and experience yet, but I was on course.

What was the difference then between the ritual and the actual? What element was present in the latter, but not in the former? At my confirmation I did not repent in my heart because I did not fully recognise God's love for me personally. So often we put the cart before the horse and mistakenly believe that if *we* love God and repent of our sins, then He will forgive us and pour out His love upon us. This is not scriptural, for mankind is not capable of making the first move to love God and repent, as the Old Testament so clearly illustrates.

Then think of Mary, who washed Jesus' feet with her tears (Luke 7) in love and repentance. Jesus said, in verse 47, that this was evidence that she *had been* loved and forgiven much. In some way she had been shown God's love, acceptance and forgiveness of herself, probably through its expression in Jesus. The first act had been God's cancelling of the debt (v.42).

> '*It was while we were still sinners that Christ died for us*' (Romans 5:8 GNB)
> '*God so loved the world that He gave his one and only Son…*' (John 3:16 NIV)

…to deliver His forgiveness. Our response, like Mary's, must be to realise and receive His 'love-acceptance-forgiveness', having been shown it either directly by God, or by other Christians. His perfect love and holiness shining into our lives illuminates our unworthiness and sinfulness, which we must confess. God then gives us an attitude of repentance as we thank and love Him in return.

> '*But if we confess our sins to God…he will forgive us…and purify us*' (1 John 1:9 GNB)

19

*'But if by the Spirit you put to death your sinful
actions, you will live'*   (Romans 8:13 GNB)

As we accept our forgiveness we are washed clean and set
in a new direction.

When God revealed His love to me, He showed me that
my fear and depression were actually a lack of trust in Him.
My unspoken prayer was, 'Now, I *will* trust you'. It was a
change of heart. I had been born again of water, in the sense
that I had become new and clean by having my sins washed
away, and I wanted to go God's way of love, joy and peace.
The process of repentance had been set in motion.

Undoubtedly, there have been times when there was great
temptation to take my eyes off Jesus, to be self-centred and
shy again, even to be depressed and fearful, yet I have heard
that still, small voice of God's Spirit telling me,

'No, you're looking in the wrong direction!
Trust me',

and his power has set me on course again.

*'Let us keep our eyes fixed on Jesus, on whom our
faith depends from beginning to end.'*

(Hebrews 12:2 GNB)

I also experienced the gift of inner healing, mental and
spiritual and was born again of the Spirit (John 3:5) I was a
new person in Christ, although at the time I only knew the
experience and not the phrases that describe it, nor did I
fully and academically understand it. Nevertheless, this was
my moment of receiving Christ in my heart (John 1:12); I
became a quickened Christian, as God's Spirit joined with
mine.

*'God's Spirit joins himself to our spirits to declare
that we are God's children'.*   (Romans 8:16 GNB)

We cannot experience the new birth until we see our need
for God's forgiveness, and this only comes through the
Spirit at work in our hearts, breaking through our barriers
and hardness. This is why conversions often take place in
times of crisis, when all our hard exterior has collapsed.

Having been born again, one is immediately a citizen of a new Kingdom, the Kingdom of God, starting now and continuing into eternity.

'The Kingdom of God is among you.'

(Luke 17:21 NEB)

A couple of months after my healing experience, I had an accident with my spectacles and had to be fitted with a new pair. Whilst sitting in semi-darkness in the treatment room, undergoing an eye-test, the optician remarked with an air of bewilderment, 'Your previous prescription is too strong for you now. You need a weaker lens. Have you been a lot more relaxed lately?' I nodded, unable to speak, amazed at the physical proof of my deliverance from fear and new life in God's love. He went on, 'It appears your eye muscles have relaxed.' I was glad that the darkness hid my blushes and wished I were bold enough to explain.

Days and weeks were now passing more swiftly than before, and suddenly we found ourselves preparing for leave to England. It was Christmas 1975. We had been in Singapore for two years. I looked forward to that leave so much. Oh to be cool and breathe fresh air again! Even though I had come to terms with life in Singapore, I still longed to return home, and to be there for Christmas was like a dream come true.

Bruce had been persuaded to carry on in the tropics for a further two years. He had talked it over with me, asking me if I would mind.

'No, I don't mind, I can face it now. Something's happened to me — I can face the future much better now, especially after a break in England.'

'Yes,' said Bruce, 'I knew something had happened to you. I've seen the change — a definite change for the better.'

'Well, I didn't like to say anything before in case...'

And then it all came out; I was able to tell Bruce, at last, how it had happened — the healing, the new birth, the peace. And now I was just about sure that it was permanent and I was determined that it would be.

21

Chapter 3
Moving On

January 1976

We arrived in England somewhat different from the people we had been when we left, two years earlier. We had changed through experiences and circumstances, none of which we would have chosen, let alone prayed for, but which nevertheless, were of great value. We had grown, matured, become more whole in body, mind and spirit. Most importantly, God had become a reality for us, and the 'Christian Way' something to be sought after, investigated and tested in a practical way.

We were in England longer than we had expected. First the boys, then Bruce, all caught the mumps, one after the other in slow succession, and there ensued a miserable time of waiting for them to recover which seemed endless and did rather dampen the holiday spirit. What with the illness, and taking advantage of relations who kindly gave us accommodation and hospitality, together with a sense of guilt at taking our parents' grandchildren away from them yet again, I realised that I was actually looking forward to our return to Singapore. If anyone had told me, two years before, that I would learn to like the place, much less call it my home, I would never have believed them, but that was really the case: I was looking forward to 'going home'.

However, I had *ideas* about that. No longer would I suffer living in a dark and dreary house with too few windows, too many ventilation-holes, and all its nasty, uninvited visitors by day and night. I had even received a visit from a Chinese vagrant, on one occasion, who took a fancy to Russell's bed!

As soon as we arrived back in Singapore, I set myself the task of finding a new house. I worked with refreshed energy, methodically, and with determination, checking the 'Houses to Let' column in the 'Straits Times' every day, 'phoning up for details, tirelessly inspecting properties. I prepared a short-list of possibilities for Bruce's boss to peruse. The answer came back, 'No, too expensive!'

Undeterred, I soldiered on, confining my investigations to rentals of S$1200 per month. I had several requirements. The new house must have air-conditioned bedrooms; a cold room would greatly reduce the chances of creepy-crawlies keeping us company at night. I also required an amah's room, so that she could 'live-in' and help out with the baby-sitting. Fortunately we could now afford this luxury. Also most important was the location; we needed to be fairly near the British schools, with at least a few Western neighbours, and a bus-stop nearby. The latter was necessary for Bruce, since the new Government-imposed 'park and ride' scheme made it extremely expensive to drive your own car into the city during rush hours.

Sure enough, the ideal house turned up. The transaction went remarkably smoothly, although not surprisingly, since I was now becoming used to relying on God in prayer to help with every detail of my life. The house in Coronation Road West met every criterion, although nothing special by Singaporean colonial standards, but we did have two bathrooms, a guest bedroom, a play-room and a balcony as bonus extras! The garden was the perfect size, not so large that it would require an expensive gardener. We even had a papaya palm, and later planted a banana tree and a coconut, too, that we retrieved from the beach.

Our land-lord, Mr. Ng, was really surprisingly obliging and made sure we were comfortable. To cap it all, I discovered that in the kampong (Malay village) behind our road, there lived a Malay woman, who had once been an amah to a friend of mine. I knew her slightly and I felt I could trust her. Thankfully she accepted my invitation to come and work for me. At last I felt able not only to cope, but to enjoy and take full advantage of the exotic life in the tropics.

By now I was happily buzzing around to all the meetings, classes and coffee-mornings that I could manage. So free was I from fear of the traffic now, that seeing our car, standing idle on the drive each day, spurred me on to take driving lessons, which were incredibly cheap. It was fortunate that my instructor came from a race of born gamblers, and had nerves of steel, for it was no mean feat when I successfully reversed round a corner, at my first attempt, into a busy Chinatown street, crammed with trishaws and hawkers as well as cars, without falling into the two-foot wide monsoon-drain which followed the kerb!

Gently, through friendships and acquaintances, the Lord was leading me on, strengthening me and equipping me for the future. One such friend was Grace Tan, a little Australian woman who had married a Chinese university lecturer and settled in Singapore with her four beautiful, almond-eyed children. She was quiet and gentle, but always on the alert for an opportunity to speak vivaciously and challengingly about her faith and the Assemblies of God church which she attended. She was continually praising the Lord, which I found a 'bit too much of a good thing', and was slightly embarrassed about. Her attitude seemed to be, 'Well, you claim to be a Christian, so I will talk openly, no holds barred, about our glorious God!' This was quite a different attitude from those who confine 'God-talk' to allotted Bible Study times and church services, or speak with hushed voices as though divulging highly secret information.

Grace brought God into everyday conversation, as though it would have been impolite to have left Him out. She had more power in her evangelism, for such it surely was, than I had hitherto seen in any other 'ordinary' Christian. She really made me think, and sowed the seeds of anticipation in my heart. It was as though she just opened the curtains a little, and let me peep through into an exciting and brightly-lit room, filled with good things. I was standing on the threshold, full of trepidation, not anxious to be right in the middle of the room, but keen to see more of it.

Eventually, Grace invited me to accompany her to a prayer-meeting. This was my first experience of people praying aloud quite freely. I was very nervous and did not participate in the expected way. During the coffee time, I noticed an old Chinese lady with a serene face that attracted me over to the corner, where she sat in a large arm-chair, dressed in the traditional black pyjama trousers and modest, floral-printed blouse. I sat down on a foot-stool at her knee and began to enquire how she was. During the short conversation that followed, she said, 'I can see you are a Child of God'.

'Wow! Could she really?' I thought. 'Am I that changed that outsiders can recognise a new family likeness?' From that time I had a growing awareness that I was part of the family of God, and that all other Christians, no matter what nationality, age, class or character, were related to me through Christ, and I to them.

* * * * *

And so, through 1976 and '77, the Lord continued to teach me in the school of life. He continued to open my mind to new possibilities, new angles on the Christian life. We continued to attend St. George's Church, and in fact became one of the families of longest standing there, because most expatriates only have one or two year contracts. As I grew closer to God, I became more aware of my sinfulness, and saying the Confession in the morning service took on a new meaning for me. The Light of Christ was shining into my dark places, showing me my sins of omission, my lack of patience, concern and tact, my meagre appreciation of all that God is, and my weak attempts at prayer.

Most of the time, though, I was uninspired by the sermons, which appeared to take the form of a moral code of ethics for wealthy businessmen. However, one Sunday we had a visiting speaker from England. He described our country as 'experiencing a post-Christian era', whilst enjoying the benefits of a Christian legacy from the past. While he spoke, the notion came to me that Singapore ought to send missionaries to England. 'They used to send missionaries all over the world', I mused, 'but now they need some for themselves. I pray that England will become a Christian nation again'.

By the autumn of 1976, being now fully mobile, with a driving licence in my wallet, I decided to take a teaching post at an international primary school. The hard facts of life were that if you enjoy the luxury of having nothing to do all day, you need money to help you fill your time. I had become sufficiently acclimatised to be able to cope with the semi-physical work that teaching demands, especially as the hours, eight o'clock until one, enabled me to retire for a shower and a siesta at the peak of the day.

Unfortunately this arrangement curtailed somewhat my Christian activities. So when I heard an announcement about a Bethel Bible Course that was to take place on Tuesday evenings at the Cathedral, I was keen to investigate. It was to be a complete over-view of the Bible, Old and New Testaments, over two years. I had no idea whether I would still be around after that length of time, but I realised my great lack of Bible knowledge, so went along to enrol.

St. Andrew's Cathedral is beautiful, all white and pale grey with tall slender columns, built by Indian convicts in colonial times, and set in a small park of tropical shrubs and trees. Its slim, white spire can be seen from many vantage points, despite the invading army of sky-scrapers which compete for pride of place. It is filled four or five times over every Sunday at its English and Mandarin services.

26

I arrived through a side-door into a large hall, running parallel to the nave, which I was amazed to find was full of people, mostly Chinese and Indians, with a few other nationalities scattered between. Mr. Ede, an Englishman who had stayed on in Singapore after the war, and made it his home, building up the famous Mandai Orchid Gardens as his business, spoke to us about the course and explained all the most difficult aspects of it — regular attendance, homework, tests, copious note-taking, all to be undertaken in, what to most people was a foreign language, English — hoping to prune out all but the keenest applicants and be left with a more manageable number. At the end of his talk, Mr. Ede asked for hands to be raised by those still eager to enrol. There were still far too many, but even a reminder about the course fee of S\$25 did little to deter their enthusiasm. It was decided to run the same course on Friday evenings as well, so as to take double the number of students. Even so, some who had been the last to apply, had to be turned away, sorrowfully, with the hope of taking part at a later date.

I attended the Tuesday course, and mine was one of the two European faces among the participants. The course was tough, stimulating and immensely beneficial, but also humbling, and any ideas I may have previously harboured, about superior Western intelligence, soon disappeared. As I made friends with some of the other students, I discovered what problems they faced as Christians in Buddhist or Hindu families, often scorned and criticized, and sometimes really spurned for their faith. I was told that some young Singaporeans would label themselves as 'Thinking', for the purposes of application forms for instance, because they were interested in Christianity but did not want to upset their parents, with whom they, as Asians, had very close bonds.

My eyes were opened to the persistence and commitment of these local Christians who numbered 4-5% of the population at that time, and amongst whom the faith was growing at a promising rate. That figure has now risen to an amazing 12%. There were even facilities for the training of Singaporeans as missionaries to neighbouring countries such as Thailand, Indonesia and the Philippines. Again, I felt myself wishing that these enthusiastic Christians would take their mission to England and rekindle her fire.

In my imagination, I pictured the small part of England that was my home. I thought of my neighbours along the main A40 where we lived. I hardly knew them, except a few by sight; we had all been so busy with our own affairs. Our house was half a mile from West Wycombe itself, a National Trust village of immense interest to tourists, both for its historical associations with the Dashwood family, and for its magnificent commanding views of the surrounding Bucks countryside. I began to pray that the Lord would raise dry bones to life in that place, and bless the people there with a knowledge of His love and power.

*****

During 1977, I started receiving teaching from quite a different source. I was asked to take over the church book-stall. This entailed not only the sale of books, but also choosing the monthly consignment from the book-shops on a 'sale-or-return' basis. This activity opened up a whole new world to me. I spent hours browsing through the shelves, amazed at the wealth of material available, trying to select the most stimulating and attractive books for our church.

One of the accepted perks with this job was that I was able to read as many of the books as I liked before I put them on sale. Through these books, many from America, I discovered what great things God was doing around the world. Best of all, I learned that a new dimension had emerged in the world-wide church — the movement of the Holy Spirit.

Apparently, in countries far away, people were actually receiving the gifts of Pentecost again, actually speaking in

28

tongues, healing, and prophecying. It was thrilling to read about. I put a few of these paperbacks on the stall.

Two or three weeks later I had a 'phone call from the vicar.

'About the book-stall, Ann, er…I've noticed some of the books are about the Holy Spirit'.

'Yes'.

'Well, er, I'd rather you didn't display them'.

'Oh, why's that then?' I asked, rather puzzled.

'Well, it's not that I disagree with it, you understand — just that it causes problems'.

'Oh?'

'Well those who think they've got *it*, really think they've *'got it'!'*

'Oh!!' It was not a very satisfactory conversation, and I for one was left with an awkward feeling, perplexed at the obvious antagonism, and determined to find out more for myself, whilst being more careful about the book-stall. I began to pray for the vicar, and to pray for renewal at St. George's. I did not understand too much about the implications of this prayer, but I knew it meant 'new life' and real, powerful, Christianity.

One Tuesday night, towards the end of the year, after I had been working on the Bible course for several weeks and grown friendly with a number of the group, we were enjoying a cup of coffee together before dispersing, when I was drawn into a brief but intriguing conversation.

'You come on Friday night, lah?' I was asked, in the colloquial Singaporean phraseology.

'No, I come on Tuesdays', I said, puzzled because she *knew* I came on Tuesdays, and the Friday course was identical.

'No, *lah*', she quietly persisted, 'after!'

'After?' I repeated.

'Afterwards, lah. *Upstairs*', she emphasised, knowingly.

'What happens upstairs?' I asked naively. She was evasive; after all, she had only heard rumours of 'goings-on', but was dying to try it for herself.

'Oh lah' (giggle-giggle). Singaporeans laugh at the slightest embarrassing situation. 'We go, next Friday', she said, smiling. 'You come and see'.

'What's it like?' I asked.

'Different', was the only reply she could offer. My curiosity was roused. What on earth was going on upstairs in the Cathedral on Friday nights? It seemed worth investigating.

*****

Chapter 4
A New Dimension

January 1978

Habits are hard to break, and I continued to go to the Bible Course on Tuesdays for several more months. In the new year of '78, our attention was arrested by a visitor from England. Trevor Dearing, an evangelist, had arrived in Singapore to conduct a month-long mission — a hectic programme of meetings had been arranged, including a brief visit to Kuala Lumpur.

The first of his meetings that I attended was on February 20th, in the ballroom of the Hilton Hotel at 7.30 pm. I went alone, travelling by taxi; what better proof that my former fears had been removed. Sunset in Singapore always happens at about 6.30 pm. In earlier days, I would not have dreamed of travelling alone, in the dark, with a strange taxi-man. I arrived at the Hilton and followed the arrows upstairs.

Entering the enormous ballroom, I found it absolutely packed with people of many races. Every row of seats was full, so there was nothing for it but to sit on the floor in a side aisle. I felt rather conspicuous, being one of very few Western people there, so I tucked myself away in a corner. There must have been an introduction with songs and prayer, but, for me, the meeting began when Trevor Dearing stood up to preach.

He spoke powerfully about the ten virgins with their lamps from Matthew 25. He told how five of them were not ready when the bridegroom arrived; they had no oil in their lamps. Only those who were ready attended the wedding-feast. The evangelist also spoke of the sheep and the goats in verse 32 of the same chapter, and challenged his audience, 'Which are you — a sheep or a goat? When the Shepherd separates them on the Judgement Day, which side will you find yourself on? Will you be like the five wise virgins and be ready, with your oil, to partake in the wedding-feast of the Lamb? How sure are you that you are saved, that you will go to heaven, that you will enjoy eternal life??!'

I was disturbed to discover that, in spite of all that had happened to me, I was not completely sure. 'Do you want to be sure?' thundered Trevor Dearing. Yes, I did. 'If you think you're a Christian, but you want to be sure, come up to the front for prayer, for re-affirming your acceptance of Christ, and receive reassurance.'

Well, I wanted reassurance, but I had hoped to receive it quietly and privately in my corner of the room. Instead, there was a long stream of people pressing forward towards the platform. This was a different kettle of fish. Did I want that special prayer enough to lay aside my pride and walk out into the central aisle. All these Asians would expect me, as a European, to know all there is about Christianity. There was a struggle inside me for a few minutes. Then I found myself walking out to join the queue. I did not care what anyone thought, only what God thought of me. I wanted to be sure.

As I waited, I could not look anywhere but straight ahead. My attention was riveted to the activity in front of the platform. As each person came forward, Trevor Dearing put his hands on their heads and prayed a short prayer. In most cases the person staggered backwards and often fell right back semi-conscious to the floor. Two assistants were standing by to catch people as they went down, so that no harm was done. I was partly amazed, partly sceptical, but undeterred as I knew what I had come for. Perhaps I passed it off as some phenomenon peculiar to Asians.

Now it was my turn. I felt the evangelist's hands on my head, and heard him praying that the Holy Spirit would come in and give me reassurance. 'Oh, he's pushing me down!' I panicked, as I felt a heavy weight on my head. 'I don't want him to push me down — it's not right!' The thoughts shouted silently in my head. 'I won't go down!' I tried to stand firm, but staggered back two or three steps under the weight. An attendant led me out to an anteroom and handed me over to a Chinese girl with a pile of pink cards. When the attendant let go of me, I realised I had to clutch on to the table in order to steady myself. My whole body was tingling.

'How do you feel?' asked the Chinese girl.

'I feel all funny,' I whispered.

'It's all right,' she said with a smile, and proceeded to ask me whether I attended church, and various questions about my spiritual growth. With the help of a pink card, she explained to me that at the laying on of hands, God was releasing the fullness of the Holy Spirit into my life, that I could expect to experience His power and gifts, and that the Spirit, who is the Teacher, would be with me always. She ticked off each point as she spoke, but my head was in a whirl, and I was not really concentrating. When she was satisfied that I had regained strength and stability, she encouraged me to return to the hall.

Trevor Dearing was about to pray for healing. 'Since there are so many people here tonight, it is not possible to pray individually with you for your ailments,' he announced. 'So if there is a part of you that needs healing, that you can put your hand on, just touch that part now, while I pray, and you *will* receive your healing.' He was so sure, so full of faith. Compared with the first part of the evening, this was easy. Everyone seemed to be touching some part of themselves. I do not know what I expected, but I put one hand on my lumbar region, and the other on my stomach, as I had been having pain in both.

I had been to visit the doctor about the severe stomach

pains which occured with annoying frequency, usually in the afternoons. He had no idea what caused them, but had prescribed some rather ineffective pills. The pain in my pelvis he diagnosed as an arthritic condition, due to carrying large babies. He thought it might improve gradually over several years, and had taken x-ray pictures to show me the weaknesses between the bones. It was not a constant pain, but a deep recurring ache, as though I had bumped downstairs on my behind!

Trevor Dearing prayed one prayer. I did not feel any immediate effect, since my ailments were only spasmodic; it was only after an interval of a few weeks that I fully realised that healing had taken place. I do not know how many of the hundreds of people were healed, but I do know that never again have I suffered from any arthritic pain, and my stomach gradually improved too, so that no more treatment was necessary.

Suddenly, I was aware of a commotion down at the front corner of the hall. A woman was screaming and crying. Some Asian pastors with Trevor Dearing were speaking in an authoritative manner to her. 'In the name of Jesus, be quiet! Jesus! Jesus!'

I did not catch all that they said, but could see that the woman was struggling as they held her arms tightly. After a few minutes, she was quiet again and sank down on the carpet.

It was a puzzling experience, but it was later explained to me that some Asian children are offered to the devil at birth. When they decide to become Christians they have to be delivered from the demons that have dwelt in them for several years. Only then do they receive peace.

After some more singing, I felt I really ought to be returning home. I was strangely restless and perplexed. I made my way out of the hall and down to the entrance to wait for a taxi. As I began to think about the evening, a feeling of great disappointment came over me. I could not understand it, but I felt petulant and irritable. Especially heavy on my heart was my experience of laying on of hands. Questions swam round in my head. 'Why did I not fall backwards like the others? Had I resisted God, or had I made a stand for truth against a confidence-trickster who had tried to push me down?' It was very confusing.

At last a taxi arrived and I was whisked away home. I did not say much to Bruce about it that night. He had been to a church council meeting and had his own thoughts.

It was not until two weeks later that I had another opportunity to attend the mission. I knew that there was to be a meeting nearer home in St. James' Church, which had been built by the Christians in the neighbourhood from their own money, so keen were they. I went early so as to get a seat.

This time, I really enjoyed singing the fresh new songs and choruses. I had never heard them before, though everyone else seemed to be familiar with them. The words were very direct and easy to understand, the melodies easy to learn. Trevor Dearing introduced his wife, Anne, who explained how, as a vicar's wife in England, she had finally overcome her pride and admitted that all was not 'plain-sailing' in her life. She had humbly gone forward for laying on of hands and prayer for the filling of the Holy Spirit. As a result she began to live a life full of power, exercising the gift of healing.

It was all beginning to make sense in my head. Things I had read about in books recently were becoming more tangible, more within my reach. The evangelist was speaking again, with authority and truth. He declared that the Lord was working with power amongst us, and that if we were to lift our right hand, as though touching an absent friend, and pray for healing and blessing, God would answer that prayer. I lifted mine thinking there could be nothing to lose, and prayed for my family. My right arm tingled from the tips of my fingers to my elbow!

As the evening drew to its close, the people began to move out of their seats and draw together, near the front of the church, singing and praying in a more worshipful way. Then, for the first time, I heard people singing in tongues. I had probably heard it on the previous occasion, but not realised with so many nationalities present. Now, however, in this smaller group, I could hear that the few Europeans were not singing in any recognisable tongue. It sounded beautiful — strange but wonderful! I was intrigued.

I had so many questions that, at the end of the service, I threaded my way through to the front and cornered the elderly canon from the Cathedral, whom I knew to be an 'ordinary' Englishman. I asked him about the phenomenon of 'falling down'.

'Oh yes', he said, 'it is a recognised sign of the activity of the Holy Spirit, and is sometimes known as being 'slain in the Spirit' or otherwise 'sleeping in the Spirit'.

'Was it all right, that I didn't fall?' I enquired.

'Ah yes,' he assured me, 'not everyone does'.

I pressed on with more questions about speaking in tongues. 'Does this gift happen to everybody?'

He confided to me that he had not used the gift until five years after he had been filled with the Spirit. 'There is no general rule', he said simply. I had the impression that he was still learning too. I went home feeling much happier in spirit that night.

I felt an excitement and anticipation growing within me, but at the same time an inner calm, that all was well. The Holy Spirit, as my teacher, was revealing, little by little, how everything fell into place. If Bruce was agitated by some problem, I was enabled to find just the right soothing words to give him. In my spirit, I stood aside from myself and listened to what I was saying — I was surprised at the new-found wisdom and knew it was not my own.

Above all, I had a deeper understanding of what Jesus had done for *me* on the cross. I was now able to complete the verse from John 3:16 GNB*:

'For God so loved the world that he gave his only

* See Chapter 2

36

Son, *so that* everyone *who believes in him may not die but have* eternal life*'.*

I could now see that if I clung to Jesus, my place in heaven was assured. He *is* all our righteousness; He is all our hope.

* * * * *

By Wednesday of the following week I was raring to go again. Being unable to explain much to Bruce about the meetings, I was keen for him to come and find out for himself what it was like.

'Shall we go together tonight?' I suggested. He did not look too keen. 'He's a marvellous preacher', I persuaded him, 'real food for the soul!'
'All right', said Bruce, 'I'll come'.

That night the meeting was in the Cathedral, being the final week of the mission. We tried to get there in good time, but arrived to find the place almost full and we were seated right at the back. We seemed to be surrounded by tone-deaf Indians with very loud voices. Bruce looked very uncomfortable.

At last the sermon began. I threw a few side-long glances at my husband during the long address, but it was difficult to discern how he was receiving it. When it was over, and the singing about to resume, I thought it wise, or kind, to say, 'Shall we go home?' There was no need to ask twice: Bruce could hardly escape outside quickly enough. We walked to the car in silence, but mentally I was praying, 'Lord, if *you* want Bruce to come again, you can make *him* want to'. Little was said between us that night.

The next day, at lunch time, the telephone rang. It was Bruce.
'What are we doing tonight, darling?'

'Well er, nothing's been planned', I replied, thinking wistfully of the mission meeting I longed to attend, and wondering what was on his mind.

'Oh, is Trevor Dearing on again?' he asked, to my great surprise.

'Yes', I said, cautiously.

'Right — we're going to it!'

'Oh, O.K. Are your sure you want to?' I was incredulous. 'What changed your mind?'

'I just decided I want to go again. See you later!' and he rang off. I realised that my prayer of the previous night had been answered. It had not even been a great petition from the heart, not carefully worded or theologically correct, but merely a simple statement of trust in God. He had honoured it.

Arriving at the cathedral that evening, I sensed a growing confidence within me, being now used to the evangelist's style, the worship, and the reactions of the congregation. It was more crowded than ever; every chair in the nave was occupied, even the extra rows at the back. We were led right up to the front, and beyond, behind the choir stalls, squeezing between the extra seats packed into every available space. Some people were already perching on the steps, but we were shown to two vacant places on a pew.

As we settled down, I realised why they had been left unoccupied. I found myself behind an enormous pillar, about four feet wide. Bruce, though, could just see round it. Not to worry, I could hear everything and feel the fellowship of those around me. We started to sing, and the evening had begun. It was thrilling as usual and I began to relax. For the first time I felt able to explore the possibilities of using my hands in worship, and I realised that I had never before clapped in church! It seemed strange at first, but I hoped that it would soon feel more natural, since it was great to express my new found freedom before the Lord.

Now came the best part of the evening — the powerful gospel message, full of hope and inspiration. I was completely absorbed all the way through, but as Trevor Dearing drew to a close, I became aware of something most unusual happening to Bruce. He was silently crying. My huge, logical, happy-go-lucky husband had been reduced to tears.

Now people were leaving their seats in ones and twos in response to the 'altar-call' as it is termed. It had been a call to repentance, on this occasion. To my amazement, Bruce stood up. He slipped out of the pew and went out to the front. From then onwards I could see nothing of him, on account of the pillars and the crowds. He was away for some time, and when he returned he looked really happy, though traces of tears could still be seen.

We stayed right to the end, and when the majority of people had gone home, we moved forward and joined with a large crowd of happy, praising worshippers, singing on and on, sometimes in tongues, and sometimes in exciting new songs, the words of which said everything we really wanted to say to God. I noticed that some held their hands out to the Lord as they sang, or just held them open in an attitude of prayer. It was a moving sight and I wished I was free enough to do likewise.

Finally we wound our way home. 'Did you really enjoy that?' I asked Bruce.

'Mm, it was great', he said enthusiastically.

'I was really surprised when you went out for prayer', I ventured.

'I just had to. I was so aware of things I had done wrong, I just wanted him to pray with me, but I didn't expect anything to happen like it did!'

'What do you mean — happen?' I asked.

'Well', he said, matter-of-factly, 'falling down like that'.

'You fell down!' I was astounded. 'You mean, you went over backwards?'

'Yes'. I think Bruce had assumed that I had watched the

proceedings. My questions just tumbled out.

'Did you fall right down on the floor?'

'Yes'.

'What did it feel like down there?'

'I don't know. I just felt all peaceful when I came round'.

'And didn't you feel him pushing you down?'

'No!'

I could hardly believe my ears. It was not just Asian hysteria, then, that caused this strange phenomenon of falling. It had actually happened to my down-to-earth, no-nonsense husband. I think this demonstrated to me God's supernatural power more than if it had happened to myself.

However, the more I thought about it, the more confused I became. I began to wonder again why it had not happened to me. I did not understand much about it, but I gathered it was the result of the complete enveloping and overpowering of the Holy Spirit. This was something that I desired as if I had a great thirst — to drink of the Holy Spirit. That night when I went to bed I prayed earnestly,

'Dear God, I'm really sorry if I resisted the power of your Spirit last week. I did not want to resist *you*, only what I suspected to be counterfeit. I know now my fears were unfounded. Please forgive me. Please take me and envelop me in your Spirit. I yield myself to you'.

With that, I fell asleep, cradled in the Lord's love.

* * * * *

That hot Singaporean night is still absolutely clear and vivid in my memory. I do not know how long I slept, maybe for an hour or less; the time was quite irrelevant. However, I do know that I woke up. This, for me, was unusual, as I always sleep very soundly now, rarely dreaming and always having difficulty waking up in the morning.

I woke up in the darkness and lay perfectly still. I was

surprised that I was awake, but was not restless, and I began to use the time in prayer, simply talking to the Lord and bringing before Him the recent bewildering events.

With my attention focused on God so completely, I felt again His love for me, and His peace deep inside me. I relaxed completely, every last ounce of resistance melted away, in a state of total 'givenness' to God.

Then, as I lay there, I felt myself being gently tipped backwards. My head was sinking below the horizontal of the bed — down, down, down, like lying full length on a see-saw and having the 'head'-end slowly lowered. A moment later, I was returned to the normal position again. The sensation had been so real that I grasped at the sheet to make sure I was really lying in bed. Of course I was.

However, I knew that the Lord had answered my prayer. He had given me the reassurance that I needed. In yielding to Him, I had rested in the Spirit. I had been over-powered by God's Holy Spirit. My whole body tingled with the thrill of the knowledge of God's loving power. Completely satisfied, I fell into a deep sleep. From that time, I realised that a new dimension had entered my life. I had (I now believe) been baptised by immersion in the Holy Spirit.

Chapter 5
Though the Vision Tarry...

10th April 1983 West Wycombe

Diana is dead!

The prayer-chain message had been telephoned through: 'Diana went to be with the Lord at ten-thirty this morning'. That was a far kinder expression — almost like announcing an appointment kept. And what will she be doing this afternoon? Without a doubt, she will be rejoicing and praising the Lord in heaven. What did Jesus say on the cross?

> *'I promise you that today you will be in Paradise with me'.*   (Luke 23:43 GNB)

None of those who know Diana have any doubts that she *is* with the Lord, and yet the words ring in our heads — Diana is dead. It's all over, all the praying for healing; praying in faith, and in little faith; in tongues, in unspoken words; in hope and in despair. We prayed for a miracle, for new life, for cleansing, for easing of pain. We prayed so much. So many people held Diana in their thoughts in varying degrees of prayer. Now the forboding, the dread, the tension is no longer with us; only the empty space remains, the gaping wound that in time will close and heal.

And yet, somehow, what my head knows, my heart fails to accept. The fact that Diana is not here anymore will not sink in, refuses to become a reality. Am I the only one who feels like this? Surely not, for all that Diana was is still with us. The fact that her body has been removed does not cancel out the effect of her life on the lives of those around her. All that she has done or said is still with us. It cannot disappear or die in the same way that her body has. Even in this simple way we see that what is of the Spirit lives on after that which is physical has withered.

15th April 1983

I believe that Diana's death was a triumph of answered prayer — 'a healed death' were the words Lorna, her soul-mate, used. The end came swiftly and painlessly without loss of dignity, less than twenty-four hours after entering hospital. She finally closed her eyes after hearing the Beatitudes read by a local pastor. Diana had prayed in her youth that her life *and* death would be a witness to God's power and love. God has answered that prayer in His own way, to the ultimate with no compromise, never swerving from the original purpose, yet always providing the strength and encouragement to stay on course, not only coping, but fighting.

Diana held out against death for more months than many had dared hope for, but as the end drew near, she was made ready to accept it, as she had accepted life, whole-heartedly. 'I am ready to go', she told Lorna, 'I am ready to cross over the Jordan. Why doesn't He take me?'

'We must just wait for His appointed time', came Lorna's reply, wise as ever.

We had prayed that she would be in church for Easter Sunday — she made it! Only a week later, to the day, she surrendered. Five days on, and we celebrate Diana's 'passover', the funeral this afternoon. It is Friday; the grief, the crowds, so different, yet strangely reminiscent of that other Good Friday; an awesome occasion and, for some, the end — for others, a new beginning, and the possibility of many beginnings. If not, for what purpose has it all been?

I cannot speak for those who see it as an end. If it is an end, then only of an episode, a chapter in the life of a village. But I *can* speak with hope and expectancy for the future.

43

How is that? It is because of the overwhelming sense of God's power, purpose and love that has pervaded the whole experience of this death, especially at the funeral.

Today has been a golden day; from early morning the unseasonably warm sun has shone down on West Wycombe from a blue, blue sky. The golden forsythias in every garden, and the daffodils at every corner, have glowed as if they would burst with joy for the spring. How strange, I muse, that everything carries on as normal, as if nothing had happened. Diana had requested golden flowers to fill the church, and our best flower arrangers had succeeded admirably. 'I don't want people to wear black', Diana had stated in her forthright manner, and many had complied with her wishes. Together with the flowers, the guests in their light and bright clothes gave a joyful air, as the sunlight streamed in through the square window panes.

So many people filled the church. Never before had I seen so many there, people of all persuasions, ranks and titles, many who had never been to church before. Diana had been at the hub of village life, living in the shop as she did, with a wide sphere of influence in the surrounding district. I was vividly reminded of a Biblical prophecy given to our prayer-group last year, from Isaiah 60.

> *'Arise, Jerusalem and shine like the sun;*
> *The glory of the Lord is shining on you!*
> *Other nations will be covered by darkness,*
> *But on you the light of the Lord will shine;*
> *The brightness of His presence will be with you.*
> *Nations will be drawn to your light,*
> *And kings to the dawning of your new day.*
> *Look around you and see what is happening.*
> *Your people are gathering to come home!*
> *Your sons will come from far away;*
> *Your daughters will be carried like children,*
> *You will see this and be filled with joy;*
> *You will tremble with excitement.'* (v.1-5 GNB)

As the service began, I did indeed tremble with excitement, and a thrill of joy swept through my body as the soloist rang out —

'I know that my Redeemer liveth'!

Such a sense of the power and holiness of God I had not felt for a very long time, not since that night in Singapore when I had prayed so earnestly for God to forgive my resistance and envelop me in His power...

Now, in very different surroundings, in a packed church at a funeral, I was experiencing that same tremendous sense of God's presence. For a moment, it was just God and me, alone, a personal encounter. I hope it was so for many others there. This revelation of God's glory to me was enough to bring the gift of tears in full flood. 'I mustn't cry!' I told myself. 'People will mistake it for tears of grief for Diana. That would give the wrong impression, for this is meant to be a service of witness. That's what Diana wanted'.

This thought carried me onward and for a while I sat relaxed and enjoyed the magnificent resurrection readings of the ASB prayer book, and the psalms of peace and assurance personally chosen by Diana.

'He spreads a table in my sight, in the presence of my foes',

we sang from Psalm 23. I was reminded of a prophetic picture the Lord had given Diana, only a few weeks before, in our prayer meeting —

'a banquet laid out, and people with grotesque faces, not eating until tomorrow'.

This certainly was a feast of her last words of witness; as her chosen hymns and passages of Scripture rang out over the congregation, one could almost hear the animated northern lilt of Diana's voice proclaiming them.

The pews being arranged 'in the round', one felt exposed and vulnerable to the gaze of others. I hardly dared look around me at the rows of faces, unfamiliar in their naked grief, the private face made public for once. However, praise the Lord, he had promised us in Isaiah 60 again:

'Your days of grief will come to an end.
I, the Lord, will be your eternal light…
Your people will all do what is right
And will possess the land forever.
I planted them, I made them,
To reveal my greatness to all'.   (v.20-21 GNB)

If I had remembered those words during the service I might not have felt such sadness and sense of panic when the coffin was carried out, accompanied by Diana's family. I caught a glimpse of her daughter's agony and my heart went out to her, and I identified with her loss. Thankfully, the next time I saw her, she was smiling, and I knew that she would cope.

Having sat near the door, I was able to slip out quickly, following the procession to the burial ground outside. I could not go close. I felt like an intruder at what was obviously the only private part of the whole occasion. As the final words of the priest were spoken, the youngest daughter stepped forward to look for the last time at the coffin. She retreated, satisfied; I wondered if she understood more than anyone else.

We all dispersed down the hill, and into the world again. 'It is finished, completed', I thought, and then, 'Why do I keep comparing this with Jesus' life?' 'Why not?' I answered myself! All through the ages God has spoken to His people through parables from daily life. He has even caused His prophets to *act out* His parables through real situations. Think of Hosea!

After Jesus had completed His work on earth and was taken into Heaven, his friends were left rather like limp rags. Little did they realise with what new life they would be revitalised. It was a small band of disciples who kept the flicker of hope fanned by constant prayer, whilst awaiting the promised Baptism of the Holy Spirit.

If *we* keep that flicker alive through prayer *now*, perhaps that same new life will come with wind and fire to our community. 'Come Holy Ghost, our souls inspire, and lighten with celestial fire'.

* * * * *

Monday 18th April 1983

This sense of the living parable is not solely in my imagination. Lorna has felt it; the vicar, too, often commended for his frankness, has made it publicly known through the parish magazine that he is bewildered, struck forcibly by the comparison with the Passover Week in Jerusalem nineteen hundred and fifty years ago. 'I cannot come to terms with it'...speaks one voice for all, 'that I will not see her again'. So final, God's power; 'the Lord gave and the Lord hath taken away — irreversible'. (Job 1:21 KJV)

And yet —

> *'I have come in order that you might have life', said*
> *Jesus, 'life in all its fulness!'*   (John 10:10 GNB)

How do we reconcile the two concepts? Perhaps it is by these words:-

> *'Except a corn of wheat fall into the ground and*
> *die, it abideth alone, but if it die, it bringeth forth*
> *much fruit'.*   (John 12:24 KJV)

Diana has requested a picture on her tombstone of a butterfly coming out of a crysalis, and the words —

> 'Even so I live'

That was her vision too — new life.

It is now three days after the funeral, and the occasion of our usual Lydia Prayer Group, a time of talking it over, and of getting it all into perspective. We recall the words of encouragement, direction and prophecy that the Lord has given us over the past few months. Things we have prayed about obediently, yet uncomprehendingly , now in

47

hindsight make more sense. That picture I received, of light shining through square window panes, came true as I sat looking at them in the church on Friday.

Last September we had been given the words —

'The cedars of Lebanon are crushed by evil, but new life will rise up out of it!'　　(Lydia 13.9.82)

Cedars — a symbol of strength! How often, recently, have people, even doctors, commented on Diana's strength. Diana was given the words —

'No morphine, no morphine, but the Balm of Gilead' (Lydia 13.9.82 Jeremiah 8:22)

Could it have meant that no medicine would save her, but God's healing would be a new resurrection body? In the week before her death, the doctors were saying, 'She must be in great pain!' But what was Diana saying? 'I have no pain!' Even *she* was amazed. The Lord had said in Hosea 7:1

'Whenever I want to heal my people again, all I can see is their wickedness'.

Is it because of our wickedness, our lack of faith, that she has died? And yet Lorna and I had felt God's word saying that she *would* die, although it was difficult to admit it even to ourselves. For Lorna, the warning came through the story of Jephthah's daughter (Judges 11:29-39) who was tragically sacrificed as the result of his rash promise of thanksgiving for victory in battle; for me, it was a strong conviction that the letter to the church at Pergamum applied to us in West Wycombe.

'…You are true to me, and you did not abandon your faith in me even during the time when Antipas my faithful witness was killed there…'

(Revelation 2:13 GNB)

Perhaps God in His omniscience knew that our faith would not be sufficient, and so warned us of her death, and compensated for it in His mercy by promising good to come out of evil.

In November, the Lord had shown us an arena filled with

people — 'multitudes in the Valley of Decision.'

There had certainly been multitudes at the funeral, and definitely some having regrets, realising that it took a funeral to bring them into church, and perhaps some making decisions. In February, we were led to pray that the people would have a personal encounter with God, resulting in repentance and new life. We were also given a picture of a golden crown, with the words —

'Though the vision tarry, it will surely come.' *

It *had* been a golden day, that Friday!

By the end of March we had the assurance that *'the banquet is ready,'* from a reading in Isaiah 25:6-8, and although we did not understand what this meant, we thanked Him for it and felt God telling us to anoint Diana with prayer. About three weeks later, I had a revealing conversation with a friend who had, herself, been in hospital where she had been praying for Diana on the day she died.

She said, 'Whilst I was praying, I heard the Lord say to me, 'Happy are they who come to the wedding-feast of the Lamb.'

'But that's wonderful!' I exclaimed. 'That confirms for us that we heard God speaking about the banquet in heaven to which He was calling Diana. It's amazing, but on the Sunday after the funeral, the Old Testament reading from the ASB Prayer Book was Isaiah 25:6-9, and the first Lesson, read out in church that day was Revelation 19:6-9 GNB:

"Happy are those who have been invited to the wedding-feast of the Lamb."'

It is obvious that the Lord has taught us to listen, and pray according to His directing, even though we often do not understand it at the time. We must continue to pray in the way He has told us, according to His will, trusting in faith, and making ourselves available to his purposes.

* * * * *

* Habakkuk 2:3

'What happens now? Where do we go from here, Lorna?' We were relaxing over a cup of tea, a week later. It was almost like the 'Cloud of the Unknowing', I thought to myself. Are we back to square one again, or are we at the bottom of a new ladder, beginning not from the ground, but from the first floor this time. And what about my writing — was it all for nothing; was my book destined to have a tragic ending? No, I must continue until I discover the Lord's purpose in all this, until the Lord provides His own final chapter — for His glory.

'You know', said Lorna, 'now that I have learned how to give my grief and hurt to the Lord, and receive His peace, I'm sure my job is to help others to do the same.'

I thought of others who were still refusing to accept the situation — who could not, would not, let her go. Was it that they did not trust God enough to let Him have her? Is that the root of the problem? Have they got an inadequate picture of God the Father? If one's earthly father has been far less than perfect and an unsatisfactory relationship has been established, then it is very difficult to automatically come into a state of absolute trust with our heavenly Father.

'We must keep on praying that renewal *will* come', we both agreed. In some churches renewal comes slowly, little by little; in others it comes rather suddenly. We do not know how God will do it here, although we found encouragement in Isaiah 60 that —

> *'When the right time comes,*
> *I will make this happen quickly.*
> *I am the Lord!'*
>
> (v22 GNB)

'We must pray that the Holy Spirit will keep a vision and a

hope before us. We must remember that directive to the church at Pergamum (Revelation 2:14-16) to turn away from idolatry and immorality', I insisted. '*There* is something positive to pray about; a word of knowledge from the Lord has pin-pointed the problem, though we do not understand it or know any details'. O Lord, that is our prayer — for the abandoning of false gods, and a re-commitment to God in the true faith.

'It's funny,' broke in Lorna, 'but now Diana's gone, I feel free. A burden has been lifted. I feel free to tackle new things. I wonder what lies ahead.'

I wonder if others, once freed from the burden in their minds, will feel free to venture into new life. I hope so. I pray so.

*****

May 1983

It is over a month since Easter. How time flies! The years seem to get shorter. Previous Easters come into vision — so often they have been times of hope, coming like a punctuation mark at the end of a cold, dreary winter. The return to unaccustomed warm, sunny days produces an air of expectancy in one's spirit, a reassurance that all is under the control of the Creator; the summer will come as promised; the pattern of seasons continues.

Of course, I write as a native of temperate climes, in the northern hemisphere. It is odd to think that in southern realms, Easter comes at the fall of the year. And in Singapore there were no distinct seasons, at least not that you would notice. One tree would be fruiting, as another was coming into leaf, and yet another having a time of rest.

This is just how it is with people. We mingle together, all at different stages in our lives, some young, some old. In our spiritual life, too, some are dormant, some bursting into new life, others bearing fruit, all growing together through the dead leaves that list aimlessly where the wind blows. When the final harvest comes, the rubbish will be swept away, and those in full leaf praised for their beauty and stature, but from those who have borne fruit will the glorious crop be gathered.

*****

Chapter 6
I Am Thirsty

April 1978 Singapore

After one's personal Easter, that is, the first or earthly one, of dying to self and coming into new birth, there must come a time of growth, a spreading of pale green leaves and the promise of fruit to come. My thoughts fly back to that Easter of 1978. Trevor Dearing had come, and gone! Was it all over? By no means! The seed had been sown and was about to be nourished into life.

A great meeting was called, an open invitation to all who had been in any way stirred or inspired by the mission. We gathered in the Cathedral and were delighted to find our new vicar, Bob, taking a leading part and working closely with Bishop Chiu.

It was proposed that a course of teaching should be undertaken by everybody who was interested in going forward with the Lord. The seven-weeks course would be known as the 'Life in the Spirit Seminar'. We were called to commit ourselves to regular attendance, daily Bible readings as set out in the course booklet, and an expectancy of the working of the Spirit in our lives. One hundred and twenty people took the decision to go ahead with it.

So many had been aroused by the mission and were eagerly seeking the 'baptism in the Spirit'. Others, like myself, had received this blessing, but had been so taken by surprise by it all that we were partially, or wholly ignorant of what was happening to us. We needed to be grounded in the biblical basis for our experience.

It was as though we had been thrown on to a huge trampoline, never having seen one before, and found ourselves bouncing up and down. Here we were, enjoying the exhilaration, feeling excited and different, but not knowing or understanding the nature of the large white canvas below us, nor how to regain momentum once it had dwindled. We needed our questions answered; we needed to know what lay ahead. Bruce and I signed on.

*****

'I just feel a great thirst! I want to know more of God. I want to hear all you have to tell me!' I told Bob. It was the first night of the course, and after a time of praise with the whole company, we had been split into about fifteen small groups and dispersed into various corners of the Cathedral. Bob had asked his group why they came. The others gave very sensible, or philosophical, answers. For myself, I thought, 'I had to come. No one could have kept me away. I want to be where the action is!'

The most marvellous aspect of this new experience of God was that Bruce and I shared it together. It did wonders for our marriage at that time. We were both on a 'spiritual high', as they say. It was a time of knowing love for one another at every level in the very ultimate of excellence.

If anyone's marriage is becoming jaded or 'lack-lustre', I advise you both to seek baptism or re-filling in the Spirit. There is no better cure! It was like being on a second honeymoon, not just a 'second-time-round' affair, but a new existence. We even looked at one another in a softer way, full of wonder, always on the brink of a laugh.

We really enjoyed reading together the short Bible passage and comment each morning. We grew in understanding and a firm foundation was set. Each week we had an assignment — to read two specified chapters from St.

John's Gospel, and the Acts of the Apostles. It was exciting and uplifting to hear the Lord speaking personally through His Word, with real meaning for us. As I turned each page, I discovered, like gems in Aladin's Cave, the words of life that fed and satisfied me —

John 15:16   *'I chose you...'*
John 14:6   *'I am the way, the truth and the life!'*
John 6:35   *'I am the Bread of life!*

I read my Bible hungrily and drew my nourishment from it.

In the fourth week of the seminars, we all met together in the Cathedral upper-room. Bob spoke to us about the expectation of the various gifts of the Spirit, (1 Corinthians 12) especially 'tongues' and his own experience of it. Then, in small groups, we prayed for the needs of those next to us. Although I was keen to receive God's gifts, especially a prayer-language, I was too shy to make 'a fool of myself', as I thought. Since no words seemed forthcoming, at least none that sounded authentic to me, I was content to wait, comforting myself with thoughts of the elderly canon who waited five years. Perhaps with hind-sight, I might have made greater effort, but who knows?

I was greatly encouraged by those who did receive this gift, since it was an outward and obvious sign of a much deeper work of the Spirit, to what extent only time would tell. The evening came to a close with a wonderful time of thanksgiving and praise for the evidence of God in our midst.

In the remaining sessions, we received follow-up teaching on the need for prayer, for strengthening, for the support of the 'Body of Christ' in fellowship, and to be alert to the taunts of the devil, trying to drag us away from our new life. We were told to expect evidence of the fruits of love, joy, peace and so on, (from Galatians 5:22-23), in our lives, as a measure of our growth in the Spirit.

For some time, Bruce and I expected the gift of tongues to come on us 'all of a sudden'. Perhaps we thought God would take control of our lips, to *make* us speak a new language. We wondered why it did not 'just happen'. As time went by it seemed less important and we accepted the idea that 'some do and some don't' pray in tongues.

* * * * *

At about this time I shifted my Bible Study night from a Tuesday to a Friday. This was due to the fact that we were cramming in extra rehearsals for a YMCA production of 'Calamity Jane'. So it was, that I found myself, one Friday evening, down at the Cathedral, sitting a 'big test' on memory verses and concepts of the Old Testament.

What a relief when it was all over — but still I had a sense of being fully-wound, alert and ready for action. No aura of tiredness or 'ready-for-home' as was the usual feeling at the end of a ninety minute session. I was reluctant to make for the car-park, and leave the friendly atmosphere of lively Christians exchanging opinions about the paper.

Then, as I drew reluctantly towards the door, I realised that this was a *Friday*. 'What *does* go on upstairs on a Friday?' I wondered. 'I might just take a look.' My feet carried me up the stairs and along a small corridor behind a hall. A smiling man was standing at the far end of the passage with a sheaf of song-sheets in his hand. He was grinning warmly at me — no escape now, unless I wanted to look foolish and flee!

I reached the end of the passage, took a song-sheet and entered the hall. I spied a seat near the door and sidled in, conscious again of being one of a minority race. Why should it matter so much? The pianist took his place and a service of Prayer and Praise began.

We sang, we prayed, we listened to marvellous testimonies from ordinary people of what the Lord had done in their lives. The service was led by Bishop Chiu who again taught us from the Bible about the work of the Holy Spirit.

During the time of deepest worship, what a joy it was to hear again the singing in tongues, so beautiful and unearthly: I wished I could join in. How strange to hear a voice proclaim a message in tongues to the assembly, but what a thrill tingled in my spine when another gave the prophetic interpretation, and I knew it was God actually speaking in our midst. When it was sadly over, I was glad I had come, and was looking forward to the next time.

After that, I tried to get to the Friday meeting as often as I could and eventually Bruce decided to come too, meeting me there after his squash game. He wished he had not delayed so long.

Here in these gatherings we felt part of a living faith. These people met together because they wanted to worship, not out of habit, or duty to a ritual. It was an 'extra' to the usual church routine of the Sunday service. And how much extra — extra power, extra reverence, extra enthusiasm, extra love, extra life — I could go on.

People could hardly wait to stand up and share how the Lord had shown His Love that week — one time, we listened to the testimony of the Police Chief, another, was the turn of a lowly soldier on National Service. Once, even *I* dared to stand up and recount the unexpected experience of sharing my faith with my head-master.

Each week there was an invitation to people to stay on, if they wished, for individual prayer for any problem. We always rose to leave immediately, Bruce anxious to return home, having been out all day. I remember, on a few occasions, I resented being hurried away, having a hankering to stay longer. I did not know why, and it certainly was not any conscious need for prayer.

Then came the night when the yearning to 'stay put' was so intense that my feet lost their power to move. Bruce made signs of leaving, but I sat tight with my eyes shut. My body felt like a dead-weight on the chair. 'I will not be wrenched away', I thought, stubbornly. I just had no inclination to leave that place whatsoever. I wanted to say, 'I am not ready to go home yet', but there was a strange lump in my throat and I could not trust myself to say anything aloud.

Bruce was non-plussed. 'Do you want to go up for prayer?' All I could do was shake my head. I wanted something, but I did not know what. I could not put it into words. How could I want more? God had given me so much already, His overwhelming love, healing, new life, His Holy Spirit; how could I not be satisfied? Wasn't that enough?

I struggled inside myself, trying to understand this feeling of desperation. I began to weep a little. By this time Bruce had beckoned to one of the leaders to come and help. I suddenly felt a hand on my shoulder and a Chinese voice saying, 'What is it you want?'

'I want, I want…', I groped for the right words. 'I want to come closer to God! I want more of Him!' I broke down and cried. 'I feel so far away!' In my grief, I felt a great gulf between God and myself. It was strange that, before I was born again, the gulf had been enormous, but I had not noticed it. Now that I *was* so much closer to God, even a short distance seemed intolerable.

Looking back, I see that occasion as one of deeper repentance. I realised my unworthiness. As we approach the holy presence of God, His light shows up our sinful separateness from Him. As we understand more of His greatness, we become more aware of our own inadequacy. It is very humbling. Our sins separate us from God, and being separated from God is a sin; sin *means* being separated from God.

Fear, doubt, worry, pride, selfishness and all wrong-doing are like great boulders that we keep putting in the way, increasing the distance as we take a step backwards, widening the gulf of separation. When we realise this, we must remember, too, the good news that we *can* approach the Father with Jesus, who takes us by the one hand, and with the other clears away those boulders and leads us through to the Holy of Holies, that we might know God.

As I tried to express my feelings to the counsellor, the tears came and washed over me, cleansing and bringing relief. The pastor, so kind and understanding, prayed that I *would* grow closer to the Lord day by day. I felt peace returning and knew I was in God's hands. I don't think Bruce understood what had happened. I tried to explain. 'I just felt so far away…'

*****

Amazingly, it was not to be long before the Lord would show me, in a very positive way, just how near He was and how concerned He was for the ordinary details of life.

Having been posted in Singapore for over four years, our long leave was well overdue. We were fully aware that the children were getting older and that we would soon have to return to England in order to settle them into the British education system.

However, things were now progressing so well in Singapore, and we had made so many good friends, that we decided to stay just one more year abroad and finally return to our native land in the summer of 1979. I had been teaching for a couple of years by now, and had saved enough money for a really good holiday. Rather than go to England for our leave, it seemed far more sensible to take advantage of being seven thousand miles away, and venture into more exotic places.

'Why not fly south, while we have the chance? It may never come again!' So we set to, planning *the* holiday of a life-time. We would go to Australia, making our way up the east-coast from Sydney to Atherton, to visit Uncle Bill and hopefully catch up with cousin Mick who had emigrated to Mt. Isa years since. Then we would hop across to New Zealand and tour the islands, north and south, in a Dormabile, then off again to Port Moresby in Papua-New Guinea and finally return via Darwin!

We sent for brochures and studied maps and time-tables.

We compared price-lists for camper-vans, and inspected temperature and rainfall charts, deciding what clothes would be needed.

'We must visit the Fox Glacier, but will it be *very* cold?'

'What will we do if we meet a kangaroo? They are very strong and might damage our car!'

Then the thunderbolt struck; our dreams collapsed. Bruce was summoned to the partner's office and told, 'We don't need you any more. The company are going to economise by employing a bachelor in your place. You will return to the U.K. office this summer!'

Chapter 7
Going Home

July 1978

Not for us - the surf-beaches of Australia, nor the wonders of Rotarua hot-springs, nor even a fleeting acquaintance with a giant kangaroo as it leaps across the road, inches from our car. No, a door had been slammed shut; any romantic ideas had to be squashed, and in their place, practical arrangements made for returning home to West Wycombe.

We wrote to our house-agent to alert him to 'no renewal of contract with our tenant after it expires in July'. 'That was good timing!' we all agreed. We reserved places in the village school for the boys, and in a very short time my inner longing to return to the English way of life had re-surfaced. The blow was further softened by the reassurance that we could use 'stop-over' air tickets, thus converting our journey home into a month's holiday en route.

Excitement grew as we re-planned our itinerary, choosing a long weekend in Bangkok, before arriving in Kashmir for a two-week stay in a luxury house-boat, personally recommended by a friend. After much debate we decided on a week's visit each to Egypt and Tunisia, as 'stepping-stones' to London.

* * * * *

The next bomb-shell to hit us concerned our house in West Wycombe. One morning a letter arrived from our agent, informing us that our tenants were refusing to move out. I was stunned.

'But it's *our* house!' I protested. 'We only let it for six months!' We had suffered so much trouble with previous tenants over the past four and a half years that we had considered a short contract a wise precaution.

Frantic correspondence ensued, with agonising delays whilst letters were flown half-way around the world. One, from a solicitor, stated, 'The Contract is worth less than the paper it is written on'. It seemed so incredibly ridiculous. We pointed out to the Wycombe Council that *we* would be made homeless.

'Can't you live with your in-laws?' they suggested. The last straw came when the Housing Department informed us that the tenants had every right to stay in the house.

Time was getting dangerously close to our time of departure. We would not be able to communicate with solicitors, agents, or anyone else for the duration of our month's holiday. We placed our problem in the Lord's hands. It was all we could do. We made three nights' bookings at the Swan in West Wycombe but after that…we had no idea! I imagined camping in a tent on my own front lawn in protest — so impossible seemed the situation.

One evening we visited our Vicar to tell him of our plans to return home. We were so grateful to him for steering us through our Christian infancy. We wondered how we would manage without his help.

'Our prayers for renewal here have been answered; you have come and we can see great possibilities of new life at St. George's — but *we* have to leave! We will never actually see it blossoming. It's very disappointing.'

'Well,' said Bob, 'not only must we pray about your house, but also that you find your new spiritual home in High Wycombe.'

'How do we do that?' we asked.

'I will write to the Fountain Trust for you, and ask them to put you in touch with a Spirit-filled church in your area.'

We had never heard of this organisation, nor of the charismatic renewal in England, in which it was involved, but it seemed like a good idea and we agreed.

* * * * *

The last few days in Coronation Road West were hectic. All the last minute arrangements for packers, shipment of boxes, and collection of tickets had to be made. Somehow it was all finally completed.

Even our amah, Ah Mui, was happily settled in new employment as a caretaker in a church! She had been as superstitious a Buddhist as they come in Singapore, sometimes visiting the Temple of Snakes, but surprisingly she was very proud of her teenage son who was a Christian and hoped to become a missionary. Shyly, she disclosed that her Andrew was teaching her to say the Lord's Prayer. Now that her life was about to change, perhaps as much as ours, she confided in me that, even if a caretaker's pay would be rather low, she was convinced that 'the church people' would 'see that I'm all right'.

At last we reached the point of no return. We had given the front-door key back to Mr. Ng and were marking time for the last few hours beside the pool at the Negara Hotel. This was where we came in! We tasted our last pineapple breakfast and our last 'fresh lime juice'. Soon we would be off on the clouds, heading for home! Mixed feelings would be an understatement!

In the midst of our excitement there was sadness too. We had shared with other expatriates our common attitudes and problems; laughed at the same jokes, at the idiosyncrasies of the Singaporeans; we had shared a common home-sickness, whether admitted or not. Now was the time for strong bonds to be broken, the hardest wrench from local and foreign friends, whom we might never see again.,

Although from the emotional, the practical, the legal and logical aspect, the situation before us looked rather grim, deep inside me I was confident that we would repossess our house. So far had I come from my previous fears of never returning to England, that now I was convinced that God wanted us to live in West Wycombe, to pray for it, to be concerned for it, to make friends there and to shine our little bit of Christ-light there.

It may not have been the peace of God exactly that I felt in my heart, but it certainly was the confidence and vision.

*****

The holiday passed all too quickly, and as it did so we became aware again that we had no idea where we would live once we arrived in England. Each day had been so crammed full of new experiences that we had given little thought to what lay ahead of us. However, our trust in God had increased as we had learned not to worry in the face of the unknown.

Sitting now in the Boeing 727, I was preparing myself for what I had long looked forward to — going home — though I would have hoped it to be in happier circumstances.

A turmoil of thoughts circled in my brain. What would confront us? Tussles with the council? Camping on our door-step? Letting ourselves into the house whilst our tenants were out and blockading ourselves in? My imagination ran riot! I had no idea what course events would take, but I was sure that God intended us to occupy our house in West Wycombe.

In no time at all we were over London. The Thames, in the rather cloudy, summer-evening light actually looked beautiful to us. Now, we were landing, rushing along the runway to a stand-still, collecting up our hand-luggage, and putting on cardigans! We were home.

I had butterflies in my tummy as we walked up the ramp to the customs. Once through with our cases, we peered through the crowds for our family. It was lovely to see them, of course, and we hugged and kissed one another, but as soon as the preliminaries were over with, I came out with the burning question.

'What about our house?'

'It's O.K. You can go in,' said dad, simply.

'You mean, it's empty? What did you do? How did you persuade them?'

The questions came flooding out. Dad was unable to give any satisfactory explanation.

'We don't know any details, but we saw the agent and he said you can resume occupation immediately!'

Without restraint, in the middle of Heathrow Airport, I exclaimed,

'Praise the Lord!'

* * * * *

Chapter 8
The Shepherd's Voice

England September 1978

Our first year home was spent in resuming old friendships and making new ones. Our poor old house needed much cleaning and re-furbishment, being rather the worse for wear after several different, or indifferent, tenants had left their marks. We could scarcely recognise our garden. It seemed to have reverted to a cross between a meadow and a rubbish dump.

The boys loved living in England again, especially Russell who had carried dim and distant memories with him all through his years abroad. His first reaction, on setting foot on home territory, was to rush down to the bottom of the garden, jump over the wall and explore the delights of the stream under the conker trees beyond. He then ran all the way back to exclaim, 'Mum, it's great!' To Mark, it was more a case of visiting a new country, and he soon learned to love the outdoor life, with no fears of snakes or dangerous centipedes. The trees in England are really meant for climbing, and you can actually sit on the grass without being attacked by vicious ants!

I set to work with enthusiasm, to be a successful and conscientious house-wife, full of refreshed energy in our invigorating climate. It was wonderful to feel cool and dry again! I was looking forward to becoming part of the neighbourhood, making local friends and praying for the breath of the Lord's Spirit to blow in our part of the world.

We had received an introductory letter from the Fountain Trust, recommending that we attend St. Andrew's Church, as it was known to be 'alive in the Spirit', and in the throes of renewal. The church was situated on the other side of town, but it was well worth the long journey, as we soon felt at home there and enjoyed the lively but ordered style of worship, and the excellent preaching and teaching.

The children soon settled into the local school and after only a few weeks Bruce found a new job which promised better opportunities for advancement and more challenging work. He also joined a Support Group for Bible-study and we took it in turns to attend a mid-week Prayer and Praise meeting. I was asked to be a 'reading-mum' and was glad of the chance to keep in close contact with the school.

Very soon, a friend invited me to join a ladies' prayer-group. I am sure she had no idea how inexperienced I was at praying, since I had spoken excitedly of miraculous answers to prayer. But praying in a group — that was different! True, there had been a prayer-chain formed during our last few weeks at St. George's and we had been fired with enthusiasm by reading 'What Happens When Women Pray' by Evelyn Christenson. The Holy Spirit had definitely begun to move there, one of the first signs being the coming together of the prayer-chain ladies on a couple of afternoons to pray for one another and the church. The meetings were awkward and stilted, but it was a start. I had uttered one prayer only, on each occasion. I have heard recently from Bob's wife that the group is now well-established and grown considerably in numbers.

On my first visit to St. Andrew's Prayer Group, I felt as if everyone expected me to pray with ease. All the others appeared to be doing so. I felt that I must make a contribution, or I would look foolish. At length, I managed to stammer out a short prayer, having thought it out, and planned it carefully for a few minutes beforehand, and screwed up enough courage to open my mouth. After a couple of sentences, I said 'Amen' with relief. It had not, on reflection, been *so* difficult or alarming after all.

After that, I grew to love the meetings more and more. Each time I attended, I was able to pray with a little more ease. The Lord had thrown me in at the deep end, but now was teaching me with loving care. I learned to concentrate on what others were saying and follow their train of thought. It was as though God gave each in turn the next words that He wanted to hear. I began to trust Him to supply more words, if I was brave enough to make a start. Sometimes, I listened to myself praying and wondered at the thoughts and ideas voiced. Of course, the growth was very gradual and I lacked confidence for quite a while.

After a while, the group decided to become members of the Lydia Prayer Fellowship. Our meeting would be preceded by a short communion service and a time of praise. Then there would follow a period of silence while we each asked the Lord to show us how He wanted us to pray. To each one, He would indicate His word either of encouragement or direction, perhaps through an imaginary picture, an idea, a word of Scripture, or a direct prophecy. It was lovely, as we learned to recognise the Shepherd's voice, how everybody received a small part of one and the same theme. We would spend the rest of the morning praying as directed, bringing before the Lord problems that seemed to hinder progress. I would leave with combined feelings of elation at knowing the presence of God, and a raging hunger for my lunch after a good morning's work.

Through such times of open and frank praying together — the exposure of the soul — strong and loving friendships were built up. Unfortunately these friends lived some distance away from my home. I sometimes felt sorry that there was no possibility of meeting them by chance in the street and giving a cheery wave. It would be such a blessing to live close to each other as a community, perhaps like the Fisherfolk at Post Green, but many people drove great distances to attend St. Andrew's, drawn by the magnetic warmth and life there, people with a living faith, eager to share it with any who would receive it. On Sundays, there would be an air of expectancy before, and during, the service, and often a sense of celebration at being part of the Lord's family.

Although we were happily finding our feet there, I was constantly aware that my particular task was to pray for my own neighbourhood. For that purpose we had been brought back to West Wycombe. Now that I was not out at work I had more time to chat over the garden fence and walk the children to school. Each time I entered the village I would pray for God's protection over it and for His light to shine there.

We had been blessed with a mild winter, and spring came early, bringing with it unexpected news from our immediate neighbours which was to force us into making an important decision. They, of course, were quite unaware of the far-reaching effects of their announcement to build an extension to the back of their house. Our first reaction was one of alarm, for the proposed building would not only block out light from our living room, but also spoil the beautiful view across the fields to West Wycombe and beyond.

We could of course object and protest about planning permission, but there *was* another solution. What about building on to our lounge at the same time, and sharing the party-wall? We were hardly ready, though, for such a major work, nor could we afford it. On the other hand, the extra seating capacity would open the way to having a support group at our house — a good way of enabling us *both* to attend! It was very tempting, but would the bank give us a loan, and would it stretch us too far? We prayed about it.

'Lord, you know our dilemma. We pray that, if it be your will for us to have a room large enough for meetings, the bank will lend us the money and that we will be able to cope with the repayments.' We left it with Him. Bruce met the bank-manager and he gave the 'go-ahead'. Our prayer changed to, 'Lord, we thank you for this extension and we pray it may be used by you, for your work and glory.'

To our amazement, it was not long befor the vicar, John, came up to us, one Sunday coffee-time, saying, 'How would you feel about leading a house-group?' And that was how we began — very green, unsure and inexperienced, but keen. Our group consisted of all those people who travelled to St. Andrew's from the west side of the town and the rural area. There were about ten of us, meeting fortnightly to talk, pray and support one another. Our first few meetings were given over to discussing the Sunday sermon and the Christian way of life. This gradually gave way to a more structured Bible Study during which we allowed God to open up our minds to the deeper meaning of His word.

There were so many opportunities for learning, so much good sound teaching, not only on Sundays, but mid-week and even a family weekend gathering. And it was not merely head-knowledge, but an opening up of the heart and spirit to the deeper possibilities of a relationship with the Lord.

One Tuesday evening, sitting with my eyes closed in a Prayer and Worship meeting, I came to the great realisation that my prayer made in Singapore Cathedral was being answered. I heard again the Chinese counsellor saying, 'What is it you want?'

'I want to come closer to God. I feel so far away', had been my reply. Over the past year the Lord *had* been drawing me closer to Him, reassuring me of His presence in all spheres of life.

There was an extra blessing too. Sometimes, whilst in the company of committed Christians praising God together, I had sung, or said, such words as 'I love you, Lord'. I had said them because I knew that was what God wanted to hear, but knowing in my heart that I did not fully understand the meaning of it, or really feel deep love for God. How could you love God, when you cannot see Him, and He is so awesome? And yet, on this Tuesday evening, I knew that I now loved God much more than a year ago. In learning to trust Him and depend on Him, and being given the example of other Christians, He was teaching me to love Him! With relief I could say 'I love you Lord' and mean it.

* * * * *

Thus 1979 had been a year of settling in, putting down roots, becoming involved. Acceptance felt good. Our house and garden were being transformed before our very eyes, from a wreck and an eyesore, into some sort of order. We ourselves were growing and taking on more responsibilities and I would have been perfectly happy, if it were not for one thing — that Bruce was not content.

Just as I had suffered a 'culture shock' on arriving in Singapore, so Bruce had suffered a set-back, spiritually and mentally, by returning to England. He was continually wishing he were still abroad, perpetuating the memories, hankering after the challenging work he used to lead and the carefree leisure time he had enjoyed. He even grumbled at our house being 'so small'.

With his discontent, he lost his joy and delight in the Lord, which in turn affected our special Spirit-filled marriage relationship which had been so precious for a few months. We did not seem to be on the same wave-length any more. I often asked the Lydia Group to pray for him, and their prayers would lift him up for a while, until he sank again. He was just like a yoyo; I was thankful that the Lord was holding the string!

By the turn of the year, I was really concerned that he was drifting away from the Lord, and being increasingly influenced by the secular world. He even lost interest in the mid-week Prayer Fellowship. Selfishly, I was pleased about that because it meant that I could attend every meeting while Bruce acted as baby-sitter. This, of course, did nothing to help the situation, but merely emphasised the rift between us.

The company began to suffer during the 'great depression' that winter, and by the spring of 1980 was struggling for survival. Bruce was made an associate to encourage him to stay on, but had to accept a four-day week, and no chance of a pay-rise. With inflation running very high, we soon began to feel the pinch. As we tightened our belts, literally, the Lord began to teach me about endurance, and the acceptance of any situation, rich or poor, difficult or easy. I prayed each week that He would help me to eke out my minimal amount of house-keeping money, and supply the clothing needs of my growing children.

No sooner did I learn to cope with one problem, than another lesson of endurance would be given me. I remember thinking that the final straw had come when the hair-drier broke down completely.

I experienced further frustration when I lost my right to drive. My international driving licence had been valid for a year since arriving in England. After that, by law, I was required to take a British driving test. Having driven for three years already, on busy city roads, I considered that one driving lesson would be quite sufficient to discover the secret of success with a British tester.

Not so! I failed dismally — made a mess of my hill-starts. I could hardly believe it. I had lost my independence! No more could I flit off wherever I chose. I was totally dependent on friends, or buses, for my travel. Was God trying to show me that I had more lessons to learn about dependence?

I had always thought that to have an independent nature was an admirable quality; that to be able to stand on one's own two feet, to ask no favours, to avoid being a burden, would be a desirable aim in life. I had been brought up on the doubtful adage, 'Neither a borrower nor a lender be'. Perhaps, however, this is a euphemistic way of saying, 'I don't need you! I am self-sufficient.' Such an attitude is totally incompatible with the concept of 'the body of Christ', in which we all need, not only to support, but also to *be* supported, by one another.

We need to learn how to receive love and help. In believing that it is more blessed to give than to receive, many have become unable to receive gratefully, humbly, like a child. The moment of receiving with joy has been reduced to a moment of wondering what to give in return. We rob the giver of his blessing.

Sometimes, because of pride, we are unable to admit our need of help. A friend says, 'Hello, how are you?' We say, 'Oh, fine thanks', when really we should be saying, 'I need your support and prayers. My life is less than it should be just now.' We need to learn how to acknowledge our dependence. The parallel is obvious: we need to learn how to depend on God.

The most dangerous old saying of all, which is also completely unscriptural, is 'God helps those who help themselves'. There may be a grain of truth in it somewhere, but it is usually misunderstood, and leads people to act according to their own inclination and plan, rather than putting their trust in God and being led by Him. God wants our complete dependence on him in every area of our lives. Jesus said —

> *'He who dwells in me, as I dwell in him, bears much fruit; for apart from me you can do nothing'*
>
> (John 15:5 NEB)

He wants to share the load with us and be yoked with us. He wants us to depend on Him for our very life —

> *'Unless you eat the flesh...and drink his blood'* (John 6:53 NEB)

That is how dependent we should be. 'Let there be no part of your life that is separate from me'. (A prophecy given at a Lydia Prayer Meeting) God wants us to realise and admit our need for Jesus, for without that we cannot be born again. He also wants us to be able to receive His love, His Son, His Spirit and His gifts, humbly, realising we did nothing to earn them, merely offering our thankful hearts in return. In that small way we will bless God; in other words we will make Him happy.

'*...as many as received him, to them gave he the power to become the sons of God*' (John 1:12 GNB)

It is of little consequence, just believing the gift is being given to us; we must reach out and take it, otherwise we are none the richer.

We, like sheep, must allow ourselves to be led to green pastures for our sustenance, safety, and well-being. Learning to recognise the Shepherd's voice will be essential if we are not to stray from the right path.

Chapter 9
Gather the Dew-Drops

January 1980

It's difficult to remember when the 'niggle' began, for it's not the sort of thing you write in a diary. One normally records actual happenings, or perhaps opinions, or even real feelings, not half-understood notions which creep into the mind uninvited, seemingly making no sense.

I have a dim memory of standing at the sink one day, peeling potatoes. I may have been praying, and if I was, it was probably for the family, and our church, primarily, but then developing into prayer for the people of West Wycombe, since that burden had stayed persistently with me. It is more likely that I had finished praying, exhausting my human efforts, and was in a state of mental quiet before the Lord, letting my mind idle on various ideas that came to me.

In the lull, whilst my fingers mechanically scraped vegetables, I heard a voice in my head saying —

'You must go to West Wycombe and pray *with* the people there'.

'What a strange idea', I consciously thought, and immediately dismissed it from my mind.

A few days later, whilst about my daily routine, the words came to me again.

'Don't pray for West Wycombe from the outside. Pray with them and amongst them!'

I was amazed at having such a thought, since nothing could be further from my inclination or plans. It just did not seem to be a feasible idea at all. Again, I shut it out of my mind, but it refused to go away for long. Every few days, I would hear these words in my head. They would sound like my thoughts, but were not in accordance with my wishes. I began to wonder if it was God talking to me. At quite unexpected times I would hear the persistent suggestion, always on the same theme.

'You should be with the church in West Wycombe.'

I began to wrestle with it. 'Now let's be practical. How can I possibly do that. I'm all tied up with activities at St. Andrew's. We've just established a flourishing new house-group. We're sure the Lord has led us into that. How can we just throw in the sponge, and let people down? Impossible!'

But the voice would return, quietly insistent.

'Go to West Wycombe!'

Still I had negative reactions. 'How can we possibly turn our backs on a church which has taught us so much? How could we manage without its support?' This was a real live church; it was exciting; it carried us along; helped us to ride the storms; helped me to endure! How could I cope without the blessings of the Lydia Group? I loved to sing in the Worship Group. Oh, it was such a silly idea. I tried to push it away; I got cross with it; I tried to forget it, but it would not go away. Still it kept coming, unremittingly:

'Go to West Wycombe…Go to West Wycombe.'

This perplexing notion seemed like one more problem that I had to endure — and endure on my own, for how could I possibly share it with Bruce, or even a friend. It would sound so stupid. Bruce was restless enough in himself, without being further unsettled by this challenge. Surely Bruce needed 'our' church as a stabilising factor in his life, I reasoned. His faith seemed flimsy, and stretched like weak elastic by now, but at least he had solid prayer support and inspired teaching on Sundays.

But reasoning did no good. The voice did not go away. By the early months of 1980 it was an almost daily occurrence.

'Go to West Wycombe. Go to West Wycombe.'

I was not convinced that it was God who was saying it. However, I knew that it was not my idea, so perhaps it was the devil, trying to upset me, trying to drag me away from a church that was so good for me, trying to undermine my confidence in spiritual matters? I said to the Lord, 'If it is the devil tormenting me, please make him stop, and leave me in peace!' The voice did not stop.

One morning it occurred to me that I had been learning to listen to God during our Lydia sessions. I had professed to believe that the words that came into our heads on those occasions were truly from God. Why not now? And since I had put my life into God's hands, wasn't it reasonable to expect to hear God's voice far more often than the devil's?

I began to explain the position to God, as if he did not know! 'Lord, St. Andrew's is such a blessing to us. It's especially good for Bruce and the boys. There is a well-organised Sunday School...If I were to go to our local church on my own, it would split up the family. I'm sure you don't want that, Lord? It would be so disruptive, and Bruce would blame me.'

'Go to West Wycombe...Go to West Wycombe.'

'Lord, I cannot expect Bruce to fling away the only pillar of support he's got! How can I explain to him that you want us to leave St. Andrew's? He wouldn't believe me!'

'Go to West Wycombe...Go to West Wycombe.'

'Lord, I owe a responsibility to my children. Lord I owe it to them to provide a good Christian education, and when they're old enough they can join the Link Club, and C.Y.F.A. too!'

'Go to West Wycombe...Go to West Wycombe.'

And so it went on, relentlessly, day by day. It was most uncomfortable, being constantly reminded of something I did not want to do. And yet I could not shrug it off. I

77

exhausted all possible excuses, but God was by no means exhausted.

'Go to West Wycombe…Go to West Wycombe.'

'Well Lord, if it's really you talking to me, then please make me want to obey you. It's no good agreeing to move, whilst not really wanting to, and feeling resentful. So please change my heart and smooth the way.'

The voice continued to whisper, but I was receiving it now with less tension, less resistance and less perplexity. At the beginning of April I was jolted to attention again by the Vicar's Easter message in the church news-letter. It was the traditional message of new life — but there was something compelling about it this time.

I re-read the letter again and again. How uncanny! Here was 'that voice' again, only in disguise. John had taken as his text:

> '*Do not cling to me, for I have not yet returned to the Father.*'   (John 20:17 NEB)

He went on to say that there is a temptation to many of us in life to cling, to be unwilling to let go. 'That very act of clinging can be a denial that life is a progression and cannot remain static. Various sentences jumped out at me from the page —

> 'It is in Jesus that I see a courageous refusal to cling
> to what was known and secure…I believe that our
> growing to maturity comes as we stop clinging to
> what we feel is safe, and are willing to prove God
> in new areas…'

There was absolutely no way that John could have been consciously speaking to me in those words, and yet I received them as God's word for me. I knew that God demands loving obedience. I wanted to obey, and as I said 'Yes' to Him, I felt a relief in my heart. I placed the weight of responsibility into God's hands, by my submission, and left him to work out the details. I said, 'Lord, O.K. I want to obey you, but I don't want to split the family. If you want us to move, then please speak to Bruce and tell him the same as

78

you're telling me.' I also had to pray that God would change my heart so much that I would really want to go to West Wycombe. Wanting to obey was one thing — wanting to go was quite another.

The trouble was that with the state Bruce was in, I just could not see him being able to listen to God, or recognise His voice. He no longer went to any Prayer and Praise meetings; he resented my leading the house-group. He was worried about his job and often wondered if there would be a pay-cheque at the end of the month, for there was so little work coming into the office. He was restless, despairing and continually grumbling. He spent his evenings indulging in escapism and fantasy in front of the television set.

Friday nights were the exception, when he would dash off to lead the local Cub Pack, only to return a couple of hours later hoarse and tired. Hard and unrewarding as this was, at least it was a family outing, for both Russell and Mark were cubs, and I was an assistant.

I remember one Friday night, I was teaching a group of half a dozen boys on the subject of 'To do my duty to God and the Queen.' A boy named Chris mentioned that he attended the West Wycombe Sunday School, so I asked him to tell about it. 'And do you sing?' I asked.

'No, we don't have any music,' he replied.

The cub meeting continued, but those words went on reverberating inside my head, like a gong. 'We don't have any music.' And quietly that inner voice said to me, 'That's your job when you go to West Wycombe.'

On several occasions there had been pleas from the church, both St. Andrew's and St. George's, for more Sunday School teachers. I had always resisted them, having some good excuse for not helping. The next time the call went out for volunteers, I still withheld my help, but my heart's response was, 'Yes maybe, but these children are not mine — mine are in West Wycombe.'

Actually, I knew very few of the children in the village, in fact very few villagers at all. I paid a weekly visit to the local shop in an effort to make friends, but it takes time for a newcomer to be accepted, especially in a village. I was usually given a cheery greeting by the manager's wife, Diana, whose ebullient nature drew customers like a magnet. She heard through a mutual friend that I was a Christian and lost no time in making it known that she was my sister in Christ. She had recently discovered she had cancer, but it made no difference to her extrovert attitude.

*****

It was during this time that the 'vision' first appeared. I was driving home from town along the A40, a very straight highway heading westwards. Before me loomed West Wycome Hill, more than a mile away, crowned by the imposing spectacle of the Dashwood Mausoleum*[1] and beyond it, the distinctive church tower of St. Lawrence with its huge golden ball held aloft for all to see.

In my mind's eye, this picture was super-imposed by another — a shining cross with bright light radiating from it. I blinked and it was gone, but reappeared on subsequent journeys until it was firmly printed on my mind. I held it before me like a candle in the dark.

Time dragged through May and June: it was a waiting time. What *was* going to happen? *Would* anything happen? What would God do? What would *Bruce* do? He still had problems. Humanly speaking, there was no light at the end of the tunnel. I was still receiving my instruction —

'Go to West Wycombe.'

I was giving the correct reply, 'Yes Lord,' but adding the

1   This hexagonal structure houses an urn which once contained the heart of Paul Whitehead, High Steward of the Hell Fire Club.

condition, 'when you tell Bruce.' I was still enduring and often felt lonely, for I was unable to off-load any more problems onto Bruce's shoulders. I often felt we were miles apart and longed to share with him the relevance of our morning Bible readings in the light of the Lord's command to 'go'. We had, for several months been using Anne S. White's 'Dayspring' as our daily commentary. On waking we would read the selected verses, and then her prophetic notes, which, being Spirit-inspired, were food for the soul as much as the Scripture was. Her book has really taught me to listen to God speaking through the Bible. During those months of waiting those readings not only gave me strength and peace, but also exhorted me to futher obedience. For example:

18th April '80 'I need an army — an army of foot-washers — wash the feet of my other children...'

25th April '80 'I go before you to prepare the way for this new ministry.'

I was still playing a full part in church life, but more and more, I had a sense of being in 'the wrong community'. When others enthused about door-to-door evangelism, I thought to myself, 'What are these people to me? My neighbours are in West Wycombe.' The readings for May were equally encouraging:

10th May '80 'My Spirit is upon you, for I have anointed you for this new ministry. Be repentant, humble, and willing to be used to proclaim my love.'

13th May '80 'Fear not, for I am preparing the hearts of those to whom you will speak.'

24th May '80 'I will open the way when the time is ripe.'

25th May '80 'When you cannot see the reason, trust me to make it clear...When I close the door it is because I will open a better one, when you are ready.'

27th May '80 'You are about to enter a new land. Keep centred in my will and my love.'

I lived for the monthly Lydia meetings during this bleak

time, looking forward to losing myself in the worship and close communion with God and my friends, though I could not tell even them what was going on in my heart. I often found comfort in recalling a prophetic vision that our vicar, John, had received. He described a desert — barren and grim, severe and demanding endurance. There was a precious blessing to be found in this desert — oil! Whilst struggling through, from dune to dune, one could occasionally find enormous cacti with exotic blooms, but most important was the fact that to stay alive, one must gather the dew-drops which collected in small crevices between the branches. John's message was simply that — gather the dew-drops. Often during that dry summer, and many times since, I have appreciated the dew-drop blessings and thanked God for small mercies.

Time and time again we would pray for Bruce, who was up in the heights one moment, down in the depths the next. One day he would amaze me by saying, 'I really felt God was in control today,' but before long he would be struggling again, shouldering all his worries himself, trying to win through under his own steam.

There was one thing that gave me hope and I clung on to it. Bruce had agreed to go on a camping holiday at Post Green in Dorset. It was to be a family week in August, run by the Fisherfolk, with evangelists Michael Barling and Bob Gordon giving the teaching morning and evening, but with plenty of free time to explore the countryside and beaches. I felt that if anything could get through to Bruce, this would be it. I could hardly wait for the summer to come, my constant hope and prayer being that the holiday would be a blessing to us all. I was spurred along by the following readings:-

6th June '80   'I will bless you and your whole family.
24th June '80 'Let me show you how this seemingly im-

possible task can be accomplished.'

16th July '80   'Your faith is growing daily through these testings which I am giving you grace to overcome. I did not promise you a life of ease but a cross to bear with me.'

26th July '80   'Your mission in life is to *encourage* others in the faith, building them up in love.' (1 Thessalonians 5:11)

Every so often I would hear a sermon preached which seemed to be so obviously saying, 'Go out from this place!' I kept waiting for Bruce to hear it too.

*****

At last, August arrived. Our plan was to pay a few days' visit to sister Pauline who lived in Cornwall, before arriving at Post Green on the Saturday. For a week beforehand we were making preparations, airing sleeping-bags, packing cases, loading the car with a hundred and one essential pieces of equipment, like a jig-saw puzzle, fitting each item into the one and only space available of its shape and size. We set off, finally, for the West Country with many prayers and much excitement and anticipation. Our morning commentary was:-

Wednesday 6th August   'Be patient. Persevere in prayer. Wait upon me to bring forth my answer of healing in this relationship.'

It was lovely to see our relatives again and we had a very happy time with them, but, in truth, I couldn't wait to reach Dorset. On the Saturday morning we were thankful that the sun was shining sufficiently to dry the dew from the tent before packing up and moving on. Eventually we were ready to go.

'Everyone in the car!'

Keys in the ignition. Feeble noises. Nothing!

'Everybody out!'

'What's the matter?' I cried in alarm.

'No idea', returned Bruce, darkly.

It seemed like an age that Bruce tinkered with that car —
bonnet up, head down. Several prayers and greasy fingers
later, Bruce tried the engine again. Hallelujah! It started!

'What was the trouble?' I asked.

'Don't know,' said Bruce, 'maybe it was damp'.

Whatever it was, I thanked God that the car was working,
but had a sneaking suspicion that we would find more
hindrances on our journey to Post Green than we had on the
way to Pauline's. With a wry smile, I prayed for the Lord's
protection over us, as we set off along the main road, recalling the commentary to our morning's reading from Psalm
37:4 —

> Saturday 9th August   'Be more conscious of me than
> of the difficulties in each situation.'

We felt no need to hurry, since it was only about a hundred miles to Post Green, and there was no need to arrive
until about 4.30 p.m. We enjoyed the country drive and visited a tank museum during the morning. It was not until after
our picnic lunch that Bruce voiced his concern about the car
again. Something, to his experienced ear and eye, was not
functioning correctly.

'We'll stop at the next garage. It may be serious,' he
warned.

Of course, we needed the type of garage that has a work-
shop and service mechanics and it soon became clear that
these were few and far between. Eventually we found one
and drove in. There was one man in attendance. In answer to
our enquiries he replied,

'Sorry sir, nobody 'ere now. All gone 'ome'.

Of course, Saturday afternoon! Who works on Saturdays
in England? We were not in work-happy Singapore now!

'There must be a garage open *somewhere*,' I insisted.
Bruce was gloomy. He was not at all sure how much further
the car would go without breaking down completely.

'I'm going back to that small garage on the left,' he decided.

'But that means back-tracking,' I remonstrated. 'Let's at least try in the right direction!'

'It's only half-a-mile back. Who knows how far the next garage is.'

So back we went. 'O Lord, please let it be open, and please let there be a mechanic there,' I pleaded.

Back at the small garage, a man came out and Bruce explained the problem. 'I think it's the alternator,' he said.

The man examined the engine for a few minutes and confirmed that was indeed the trouble. 'I'll go and see if we have the type you need on the premises. I believe we only have one.'

Whilst he went to look inside, we anxiously prayed again. A few moments later he reappeared, alternator in hand. 'You're lucky,' he said. 'We only had one and it's the right sort. The trouble is, the mechanic who knows how to fit it has just gone home. Hang on. I'll give him a ring and ask if he minds coming back again…'

More prayers and anxious waiting. We looked up hopefully as the man appeared yet again. 'His wife says he's just popped out to have a flutter on the horses, but she'll give him the message when he gets home. Do you want to wait?'

I looked at my watch. It was 2.30 p.m. Although we still had a good hour's journey ahead of us, we had no alternative but to wait. The children and the dog were unpacked from the car and warned to expect a long wait.

My imagination began to run wild. 'How *long* does a man spend at the races on a Saturday afternoon with his new pay packet in his pocket? We could be here for *hours*!' It certainly looked as though the devil was doing all he could to delay our arrival at Post Green. 'If he's trying this hard to stop us getting there, there must be a good reason for it,' I thought to myself. 'It must mean that the Lord has something great in store for us. Well, praise the Lord that we are on *His* side.'

After an hour we knew every inch of that forecourt; Snoopy had sniffed every blade of grass, and we had admired the view for so long that it looked quite ordinary after all. But when a car drew up and a mechanic jumped out, we realised the wait had been worthwhile.

The man began at once. It was a lengthy job, but it did not seem so bad now that we could see some action. 'You were lucky we had the alternator in stock,' he remarked.

'Mm,' I thought, 'not luck — another battle won for the Lord's side.'

*****

We arrived very late at the campsite. There was just time to pitch our tents and consume a hurried meal before the Welcome Meeting began. We had so much to praise God for that evening that it was good to have the opportunity to express our relief in the worship-time. During the evening, I prayed that Bruce would really listen to, and accept, the teaching that week, and that it would be a turning point for him. I prayed too that the children would enjoy and benefit from the week, and that Mark's cold would not develop into the usual bronchial asthma. I felt hopeful as we returned to our sleeping bags after our late night cocoa by torch light.

Next morning we explored the site, admiring the unfamiliar wild flowers and heather, so different from the flora of our own chalk hills. Unfortunately the weather was showery and deteriorated as the days went by. Thankfully it improved in the afternoons which were free for sightseeing, and on the free-day, Wednesday, we spent a lovely time at the beach in the sunshine.

However, between times the storms were heavy. The four of us crouched in our ridge-tent, playing card-games, listening to thunder and lightning. I prayed hard that the tent would not leak; it would only take one shoulder rubbing against the canvas to cause the rain to come pouring in. Thank God, we kept dry, but others were not so fortunate, even those in caravans. Wet bedding and clothing was draped around the large marquee with every available source of heating, for a couple of days. It was difficult to keep our feet dry, but miraculously, Mark's cold remained under control.

I found the morning seminars very sound and enriching — amusing too, and Bruce showed no signs of playing truant. The children enjoyed the junior meetings in the mornings, whilst in the evenings we all attended the big meeting together. I had a surprise on the second evening. During a time of prayer, the preacher was given a Word of Knowledge from the Holy Spirit. He said, 'There is someone here who is very lonely. The Lord does not want you to feel alone. If you stay behind at the end, I will pray with you.' It hit me like a bullet. I had spent so much time praying for the family, but I had not expected to have my own problem ministered to. At that moment, however, I knew that the Lord had spoken to me. I was amazed and thankful that God loved me so much as to pin-point *my* need as well.

When everyone had retired to their tents, and Bruce had led the boys off to bed, I poured my heart out to the counsellor — all about how alone I felt, how I was unable to share my problems with my husband nor gain support from him, how we were on different wave-lengths. Michael's words were very comforting. He explained how Jesus *knows* what it is like to be alone; in coping with the Cross He was absolutely alone, even separated from His Father by the sins of the world for a time; he has trodden the lonely road before us, understands exactly what it is like and can share it with us now.

That was a tremendous comfort to me. I recalled a night when I had burst into tears and told Bruce, 'I feel so alone!' He could not understand, but now I knew that Jesus did. What strength and ability to cope I derived from that.

Later, over steaming mugs of cocoa, we sat in the awning in the dark and I was able to explain a little about it to Bruce. It seemed an ideal time for talking and we began to open our hearts a little to each other. My morning's reading had included the line:-

Monday 11th August: *'My love sets you free.'*
and the next morning we read:-

Tuesday 12th August: *'Bear one another's burdens and so fulfil the law of Christ'*   (Galatians 6:2 GNB)

It became part of the routine to end the day like this, drawing closer each evening and as the week wore on I became aware that several of my prayers for Bruce were being answered. One evening he told me that he realised what a waste of time it was to watch so much T.V. and he was determined to make better use of his time. Another evening he expressed a wish to instigate family prayers after breakfast each day. I had long wished that we could resume praying together which we had tried in fits and starts in the past.

Bruce also disclosed that he had had an unusual dream. He explained that he had seen a fish floating near the surface of the water, about to die. Then suddenly it revived and swam off into the deeps again. 'I think God is reviving me like the fish and giving me another chance!' It was obvious that the message was very real and important to Bruce and I thanked the Lord for it.

Most exciting of all, though, were the ideas that Bruce revealed on our last evening. So exciting were they that I was not able to concentrate or remember exactly what he said, but he expressed his first feelings of concern about the people of West Wycombe, and I knew that he had become aware that there was work to be done there. I knew God was working on Bruce and I determined to be patient a little longer.

In spite of all the activities, we found it a very relaxing and uplifting week. We even made time to seek out Bob Gordon and ask his advice and encouragement for our newly made resolutions. In particular, I had to ask him about a certain burning and recurring question concerning 'tongues'.

Since our 'Life in the Spirit' seminars in Singapore, I had tried not to think about this gift too much, or to worry myself about it. I did not especially see the need for it personally. However, during the intervening couple of years, I had become increasingly disturbed by the opinions of other Christians, regarding the necessity of this gift. It appeared that there was a large body of opinion that regarded 'tongues' as the 'proof' that baptism in the Spirit had taken place. I did not feel that I needed that particular proof, because I had assurance of the 'baptism' in other ways — a new love and understanding of the Bible, a de-scaling of my spiritual eyes, more freedom in prayer and worship, and a new God-given caring about other people.

Even so, I fell prey to doubts occasionally. A friend had also advised that, 'You should really pray for the gift of tongues, you know, as it is such a powerful kind of prayer.' Now this seemed a much more important reason for wanting it, but only served to disturb my thoughts even more. It was on this issue that I tackled Bob.

He was most reassuring, saying that there were no grounds for stating categorically that everyone baptised in the Spirit must speak in tongues. 'However,' he said, 'it is certainly a gift of great value for the building up of your own self, and of the church, in others words, edification.' I admitted that, to be honest, I did wish that I had the gift, for I was ready to receive any gift that God wanted to offer to me. So Bob prayed for the Lord's encouragement for both of us, including the receiving of 'tongues'. My mind was at peace at last on this issue, and I decided to earnestly expect an answer to the prayer.

As always, the holiday came to an end before we would have wished. However, I always look forward to going home, feeling that the daily round, the common task, will be much more enjoyable with the newly gained vigour and refreshment of spirit, effected by the change and rest.

Once home, we began joyfully to put into practice the decisions we had made, sharing a common goal once more. We both looked forward to the first Prayer and Praise evening of the autumn and went along together to share our holiday experiences of 'renewal'.

We had some very important prophecies from Anne White in our morning readings, some of which were only fully appreciated with hind-sight!*

18th August	'The new doorway that I am opening is not an easy one, but it will be rewarding.'
19th August	'I have new plans for your life — some beyond your furthest hopes.'
*25th August	'Do not fear those who worship the devil.';
*29th August	'You are to write in obedience. The truth which has set you free will be made known in others.'
1st Sept.	'Rest in me now...I have brought you through the turmoil and the storm has now abated. I set you in green pastures.'
7th Sept.	'Let the Word of God be spoken through your lips. You will be amazed to see their response.'

I still had the task of bearing a secret casket, the contents of which I could not divulge, but the weight of it was not so great now, as I could sense that Bruce was about to discover it, like the uncovering of a hidden package on Christmas morning. I kept praying that he would, so that we could share the adventure together.

Chapter 10
No Turning Back

September 1980

I looked up at Bruce in amazement, leaving my half-bitten sandwich on its plate. '*What* did you say?' I knew I must ask him to repeat it, lest I may have imagined it, or heard only what I wanted to hear. I knew I must beware of putting my words into his mouth.

Bruce cautiously repeated what he had just said, quite unaware of the crisis of emotions and thoughts welling up inside *me*, but conscious that he may have said something important. 'I think,' he said, 'that the Lord's got work for us to do in West Wycombe. He wants us to get involved.'

My heart was pounding, but still I tried not to get too excited. Perhaps Bruce meant to frequent the pub more regularly, or to clear the footpaths.

I had been sharing with Bruce, who had come home for lunch, some of the more sensational snippets of news from the Lydia meeting that very morning. I told him we had been praying for a household in the St. Andrew's parish who were thought to be dabbling in witchcraft. I mentioned that I had heard that West Wycombe holds a reputation for having been an occult site in the past, and that some say there is still a local coven.

'I think we should spread a little light there,' went on Bruce, 'join in some activities, even visit the church on the hill.'

This is *it!* This *must* be it! I thought. I had one more

question though. 'Is this your idea, or do you think God is telling you this?'

'I think it's from the Lord,' he answered.

'Well, that's just marvellous,' I enthused. 'He's been telling me the very same thing and I've been praying that he would tell you too!'

It was a wonderful relief to talk about it at last but I had to take care; the whole idea was new to Bruce. It would never do to put him off with my over-enthusiasm whilst he was still getting used to it and wondering how it would work out.

It was Anne White who eased the situation for us. From that time onwards our morning readings took on a special meaning and encouragement for both of us. In fact that very day's reading had been from Psalm 34:4 GNB:

'I sought the Lord and he answered me'.

followed by the commentary: 'I can deliver your loved one today' — the very day of Bruce's revelation.

The next morning, Thursday 11th September, our reading was from Philippians 2:13 GNB:

'For God is at work in you, both to will and to work for his good pleasure.'

Commentary — 'You are my beloved. When you obey my commands, I am abiding within you to work out the details of your life. You need fear nothing but the loss of Me, for I can bring good out of evil and transform this situation.'

From this promise, we understood that God was going to make us willing and able to obey his purpose, if we would surrender our wills to Him in trust.

Out of Friday's reading of Hebrews 5:14 came the prophecy —

'You are to lead others away from the power of the enemy.'

Sunday 14.9.80 (Comment on Luke 9:62) '...you will need endurance...There can be no turning back for those who are totally committed to Me for I am coming sooner than you think. Have faith in my word. Be constant in the face of dangers and troubles. Be centred in me.'

On the same day, there came a message to us from the sermon — to be a strong partnership. That seemed much more possible now than at any other time since leaving Singapore.

*****

In the ensuing weeks we began to see evidence of God gently loosening our ties. The following Wednesday evening, our Support Group met again after the summer break. Unfortunately three couples were in the throes of moving house and it appeared unlikely that they would continue to attend meetings. Ivan, our missionary friend from the Wycliffe Centre, notified us that he was off to South America very soon, and Sylvia had only a couple more months before her baby was due; her occasional cat-naps during our bible-studies were evidence that she was really too tired to concentrate. I was quite despondent that night as I retired to bed, feeling that I was fighting for the group's survival. My pride was suffering — surely it was my responsibility, to hold this group togther, as a measure of my success?...

> Thursday 18.9.80   1 Corinthians 15:55-58:
> *'O death where is thy victory?'* (v.55 RSV)
> A.W.'s Comment: 'Have you not fully recog-
> nised my victory over death?...You are still
> holding on to your desire...because of your pride.
> You prayed and things did not happen as you
> wanted. This is the sting of death. Release this
> person (*¹ group) to me...'

(*¹ my interpretation)

I realised that the Lord was speaking to me about the death of my house-group, which I knew was slipping away fast. He was saying, 'Release the Support Group to me. Be comforted. Nothing you do in the Lord's service is ever useless (v.58 GNB).' He was bringing this area of my life gently to an end, easing away the members, one or two at a time, not by unpleasantness or disagreement, but by natural events. God was working out his loving plan and it was senseless for me to hinder Him.

Bruce was taking it all very well. He did not appear to have as many doubts as I had had at first — perhaps because we both shared the vision and confirmed it for one another now. All the same, we did have an uneasiness about our own inadequacy to cope with the situation ahead. We felt as though we were soon to be tipped out of the cradle and set on our own shaky feet in the middle of a vast and dangerous world. We always fear the unknown, even when a craving for adventure spurs us on. Bruce wanted to know what was the purpose of it all and what would be our task in our new community. 'Why?' and 'What for?' were our burning questions.

> Tuesday 23.9.80   Ephesians 5:17 GNB — *'Do not be foolish, but understand what the will of the Lord is.'*

Now every sermon we heard in church held a secret prophetic message for us, generally on the theme 'Go!' On Sunday 28th, John preached, 'When the Lord tells you to go, do not fear. The Lord will show you what to do.'

'Does John *know* what we're planning to do?' I thought, incredulously. I was sure Bruce had not told him, as we were both feeling a little guilty about the severance of loyalties. Our reading that morning had been 1 Corinthians 2:1-10, and from it came Anne White's inspiring exhortation —

'...Proclaim the Father's love, that none can fully

94

comprehend except by my Spirit. *Be* my love,
ministering to the mature who have worshipped the
intellect and failed to see or hear or transmit My
all-encompassing love...'

'Proclaim My love' — that was fairly straight forward, but
'Be My love' was impossible in our own strength, especially
as outsiders breaking into a close village community. We
prayed about it, of course.

Further instructions came on:

Thursday 2.10.80 — 'Repent, study My word,
pray, have fellowship with Me and others of My
children.' In other words, we were to prepare
ourselves well and make sure we were clean
instruments.

Sunday 5.10.80 — *'...I chose you and appointed
you that you should go and bear fruit.'* (John 15:16
GNB)

A.W. warned: 'When you are used by Me to
help others, do not take the glory to yourself or the
fruit will be tainted.'

Monday 6.10.80 — *'... We know and believe the
love God has for us...'* (1 John 4:16)

The Lord said to me: 'My perfect love will cast
out your fear.'

Did I still have a sub-conscious fear — fear of the
unknown, of being out on a limb, or literally 'out in the
sticks!?' Probably we were both affected by the weird
rumours abounding in the locality, such as:

'and don't let anyone tell you there's not a passage
from West Wycombe hill to 'the house', because I
know there is — I've been in it!'

This is a rural area, not part of High Wycombe team
ministries, but a sprawling parish of country lanes, new
pockets of development, unfriendly main roads, besides the
actual village of olde-worlde properties huddling together in
disarray, as though for protection, turning their backs on the
A40 so rudely thrusting its way through their midst. The

High Street is merely a face presented to the world. Behind this rather bleak and traffic-polluted facade lies the true village, unseen and unknown to those who speed by in cars and buses. But get out of your car and explore the back alleys and hidden paths and discover the real life of the place, the families, people with stories to tell of days gone by, of customs and feuds, of superstitions and prejudices.

'What is this village really like?' I wondered. 'Can one believe all that one hears of the notorious Sir Francis Dashwood of history,[2] whose family still live here in the 'big House' in the park?' Or were the rumours merely perpetuated for commercial reasons, since pandering to the modern interest in the occult and the vices of the gentry can be highly profitable? There was no doubt that the one-time Lord of the Manor, and indeed Chancellor of the Exchequer, had been involved in very curious pastimes, together with certain parliamentary friends, and books about their Hell Fire Club in West Wycombe caves are readily available. 'How much influence has filtered through the generations to remain within the very bed-rock of our community?'

I realised that I was now really keen to know and understand the locality to which God had sent us home. Further light was shed with Tuesday's reading:-

Tuesday 7.10.80 — A.W.'s comment on Luke 15:7:

'I came to save the lost sheep. Let me make a pathway to this one who needs to be loved…She is straying because of past circumstances that have made her a victim of the sins of others…'

My interpretation — 'This one who needs to be loved' is the

[2] Sir Francis Dashwood, 2nd Baronet, 1708-1781

village of West Wycombe. 'Past circumstances' refers to the grip of rumoured and actual evil of its history which still holds an influence over people's minds, whether realised or not.

* * * * *

We began to talk over the matter of timing. When should we leave St. Andrew's? What would be the most convenient date? We were already into October and preparing for an outreach programme in November, for which we were well keyed up and praying for converts. Then December would bring the Christmas festivities. We would not choose to leave 'home' before celebrating with our friends! 'Well let's make January our goal,' we said. 'That seems like an appropriate time for new beginnings.' 'Yes,' I thought, 'it won't be so difficult to leave in January.'

I had been very busy, as usual. So many activities were packed into my week that there was scarcely time to do the housework properly, let alone tend the garden. Overcome by conscience, both that the garden needed attention, and that my waist-line was larger than necessary, I had been skipping a few meals. I happened to let this fact slip whilst in conversation with Bruce. He scolded me for not eating regularly.

'Oh I have enough food!' I replied cheerily. I would have expected him to applaud my feeble attempt to diet since he often teases me about my 'spare tyres.' To myself I said, 'My food is the Word of God!' I was sure I had read that somewhere in the Bible and it seemed to fit the current situation.

The next day I was thumbing through my Bible, when my attention was caught by the word 'food'. I stopped flicking the pages over, thinking 'Oh, what *does* the Bible say about food?' It was in the gospel of John, chapter 4, verse 32 and 34.

> *'My food,'* Jesus said to them, *'is to obey the will of the one who sent me and to finish the work he gave me to do.'*

Well, it was not the reference I expected, but it certainly was relevant. I found myself reading on, my eyes drawn to the next verse, for it was really speaking to me.

> *'You have a saying, 'four more months and then the harvest. But I tell you, take a good look at the fields, the crops are now ripe and ready to be harvested!'* (John 4:35 GNB)

Four more months! I counted up. From the time we had both recognised God's call to go to West Wycombe, the beginning of September, until the beginning of January was exactly four months!

> 'But I tell you the harvest is ready now — now — now!

God was saying, 'You cannot wait that long. There is an urgent need for you to go as soon as you can.' I read on to the end of the paragraph, finding encouraging words of promise in v.36.

> *'The man who reaps the harvest is being paid and gathers the crops for eternal life; so the man who sows and the man who reaps will be glad together.'*

I sensed the plan and purpose of God being worked out, no man being given the whole task to perform, but each a part of the whole, in a holy co-operative. It was very exciting.

Bruce took it more calmly than I had, but we both accepted the urgency and the need to abandon our former plan. We began to look positively for an opportunity to speak to John, though it was not that straightforward. We could not just walk up to the vicar and say, 'We're leaving!'

> Amazingly our reading for Wednesday 8.10.80 was Luke 14:23 GNB — *'Go out to the country roads and lanes and make the people come in, so that my house may be full.'*

Thursday 9.10.80 1 Corinthians 12:27 GNB —
'You are the body of Christ.' A.W.'s comment:
'Share your difficulties with one another in your
prayer group...Shared burdens become
lighter...Then rejoice as you go your separate
ways.'

We discovered that John was planning to attend our next
Support Group meeting. That would be our chance to break
the news. We felt it only courtesy to tell him first, before
anyone else. Unfortunately, due to pressure of commitments, John had to postpone his visit, but promised
faithfully to come on the very next occasion because he
wanted to discuss arrangements for the November mission.

We continued to pray and prepare ourselves, whilst being
constantly exhorted to praise and stay close to God. I do not
deny that we still had doubts, especially as rumours were
reaching our ears about West Wycombe in a rather uncanny
way. Isn't it odd how gossip is very seldom good? We even
heard, on the grapevine, that some church members were
discontented, and that the few committed Christians there
were being criticized for proclaiming their new life in the
Spirit. I was glad to hear that there was indeed a nucleus of
commitment and a spark of renewal. It was my aim to find it
and work with it no matter what the difficulties.

Friday 10.10.80 — 1 Thessalonians 5:16
'Rejoice always.'
A.W.'s comment: 'Do not quench the Spirit with
your doubts and self-pity, but rejoice in all
circumstances, even those that seem to be evil, for I
can bring good out of them...test the spirits!'

Saturday 11.10.80 — 2 Thessalonians 3:3 *'The
Lord is faithful...he will strengthen and guard you
from evil.'*
A.W.: '...I will comfort you when others
condemn you falsely.'

Friday 17.10.80 'The devil is deceiving even
leaders in the church with his subtle heresies. He is

dividing husbands and wives, parents and children.'

We had several readings about the purpose of the family in God's plan. We were instructed to pray for husbands to take their proper place as spiritual head, subject to Christ. I think this was not only a word for Bruce, but also an area of prayer for our new community.

At the same time I became aware of the vulnerability of women to the deception of the devil, as warned by Paul, and the need for a wife to be 'covered' by her husband as her protection. I was truly thankful that I had a Christian husband and that he was in agreement with our proposed adventure. He was much more confident of late, with a new purpose and vision, even though the situation in the office was as bad as ever.

> Monday 20.10.80 A.W.'s comment: 'Remain steadfast in prayer and I shall overcome the evil assault of the enemy: I shall vindicate my plan.'

> Wednesday 29.10.80 — Our Support Group day dawned at last. What would the Lord say to us today?

> Through A.W. He said: 'Pray as if to open prison doors. Be prayer warriors to release my Power...remain constant until the enemy yields. *Claim dominion over his deceits*'.

John came to our group that night. The meeting was given over totally to preparation for the mission. We were told what to expect of the evangelistic team and of the programme for the coffee evenings that they would lead in various homes, including ours. Every detail was discussed, about sharing our faith and leading seekers to conversion.

John was extremely patient and did not appear to be the least bit hurried. 'Now is there anything else?' he asked. Yes, some more queries came up and were dealt with. 'Anything else?' came John's question again and again, until no one could think of a single point to raise. He didn't appear to want to go home. He just kept sitting there on the settee saying 'Anything else?' until it began to prick through my skin.

'Why does he want us to say something else,' I wondered. 'Is this the chance we've been waiting for? Is John in fact forcing our hand.' Once again I thought suspiciously, 'Does John actually know our plans?'

I looked at Bruce on my left and raised my eyebrows. It was obvious that he had the same thought. After a couple of secret nods, I said,

'Yes John, there is something else, but it's nothing to do with the mission.'

'Go ahead then,' he said.

There seemed no point in wasting words. I came straight to the point. 'We think the Lord is telling us to move to St. Lawrence's Church.'

John took the news predictably calmly and thoughtfully, and with the slightly amused look he always wore. Perhaps he thought it was a sudden decision, or impulse, or the result of dissatisfaction with his church, but as we went on to share the telling of our saga, trying not to garble the version, his look turned to one which could only be accompanied by the words, 'You don't say!'

Especially incredible to him were the times when we had heard him telling us to 'Go!' from the pulpit. He had no idea what tender parts that double-edged sword had pierced.*[3] We brought our story to a close with the words from John 4:

'I tell you the harvest is ready now.'

'Well,' said John with cool-headed efficiency. 'You had better not waste any time.'

'But what about the mission,' we protested, 'we can't go before that, can we?'

Calmly John took out his diary. 'Let's see, your coffee evening is on the 26th November, four weeks from today. The Sunday after that will be the climax to the week, with the visiting speaker, Barry Kissell, giving his evangelistic

---

*[3] Hebrews 4:12

message to the masses. Not a very suitable day for your farewell. It will have to be the Sunday before — our Gift Day — highly appropriate. You can both say a few words of explanation about giving yourselves to the Lord's work — then a prayer of commissioning — it all fits in. That's settled then! I'll ring your new vicar to explain why you're coming. I must be getting home. It's late!'

After John had departed, Bruce and I looked numbly at each other. 'Well — that's it', we both agreed. 'There's no turning back now.'

> Thursday 30.10.80 — *'If two of you agree about anything you pray for, it will be done for you.'* (Matthew 18:19-20 GNB)

* * * * *

> 2.11.80 Psalm 37:3 — *'Trust in the Lord and do good; so you will dwell in the land and enjoy security.'*
>
> Commentary — 'Now that you have prayed deeply about this problem, leave it in my hands. Do not be impatient. Do the small task I have given you joyfully. Stay committed to me. I will act.'

This reading led us to take stock and ask ourselves, 'In a nutshell, what is God saying?' Basically, it boiled down to two things — to love and to pray, whole-heartedly, through whatever tasks or activities came our way. Our prayer project was to resist and stifle the enemy, so clearing the way for the renewing life of the Holy Spirit.

13.11.80 We were given that tremendous passage from Romans 8:38-39 GNB:

> *'neither death, nor life, nor angels, nor principalities, nor things present, nor things to come, nor powers, nor height, nor depth, nor anything else in all creation, will be able to separate us from the love of God in Christ Jesus our Lord.'*

Even though we were about to separate ourselves from a

church which had been a firm foundation beneath our feet, even so, there was no need to despair. Perhaps we had relied on this human rock too much. The time had come to put into practice the lessons learnt about dependence on the Lord. We needed to trust even more in God himself, to know that we could turn direct to Him in all circumstances.

I was really becoming excited about the move, and was bursting to tell Diana of our coming, but was determined not to let the 'cat out of the bag' before John had spoken to our new vicar. However, the feeling about the Sunday School was growing within me, and I could not resist making some 'innocent' enquiries.

The shop was Diana's centre of evangelism. She was not in the least bashful or self-conscious about speaking plainly. It was quite usual to hear her praising the Lord and telling people 'How great He is!' It was easy therefore, when she mentioned the Sunday School one day, to casually ask, 'Do you have enough teachers for the children?'

'Oh yes, we're all right,' she jumped to defend the situation. I said, 'Oh good,' as I accepted my change and a chocolate bar. On my way home, I thought, 'It's just a musician they need then.' I was quite used to playing my guitar to accompany children's songs at school, and was keen to offer my small talent, such as it was, for the children's benefit.

At last we got word that John had made our introductions by phone. I could not wait to spill the beans personally, and knew I must contact Diana. I rang her. 'Can I come round to see you. I have something to tell you.' She was quick to realise this was somewhat more than a grocery order.

'Yes, come after tea,' she replied.

'What — today?'

'Yes, I can't wait any longer than that!'

A little while later I arrived at the Post Office door. Diana opened up, and I followed her through to the back, squeezing between piles of boxes and the deep-freeze, through a short passage to the dining room.

'Sit down,' she said, in her blunt way, indicating a chair opposite hers at the table. We sat and faced each other. I hesitated, wondering what to say first. Her husband walked through on his way to the lounge.

I said,

'It's trying to rain now, quite nasty it is.' He disappeared out of sight, and Diana remonstrated.

'Look, you didn't come here to talk about the weather! Get on with it!'

'All right. We're coming to West Wycombe.'

'What do you mean?'

'We're coming to St. Lawrence's. We're joining you.' I went on to explain it all, how the Lord had told us to come, and how we were to pray with the Christians there. We both agreed that the greatest thing was the evidence that the Lord had his plans for West Wycombe — yes, even this small Chiltern village of West Wycombe.

'And there's something else,' I continued. 'I think the Lord's telling me to offer my help with the Sunday School.'

'Great!' exclaimed Diana. 'There's an answer to prayer. We needed someone to take over the Sunday School.'

'Hey, wait a minute,' came my surprised reply, 'I thought you had enough teachers. I only offered to *help*.'

'Well, Lorna and I have been taking the children's classes for some time now and we both feel we have no more to give. We nearly gave it up back in April, but the Lord said 'carry on a little longer'. So we did and we've been praying ever since for someone to take our place.'

I was amazed. The timing fitted so well with the Lord's first word to me at the Cub meeting.

'Diana...I don't really feel adequate to take over, but since it seems like the Lord's in charge of all this, I had better agree and leave it in His hands. I would feel happier teaching the older age-group.'

'That's just fine — the little 'uns are already taken care of. We'll hand over to you straight after Christmas.'

* * * * *

104

On Sunday November 23rd, we woke bright and early as one does on a special day. This was not only St. Andrew's Gift Day, and the start of the Barry Kissell mission, but also our own commissioning day, our 'swan song'. We would be expected to 'say a few words.' It was enough to give me butterflies in the tummy. Our morning reading was, of course, ideal for the occasion.

> Sunday 23.11.80 — 1 Peter 4:10 GNB *'As each has received a gift, employ it for one another.'*
> Comment: '...Do all that you are led by My Spirit to undertake...in humility, not claiming the glory for yourself,' even 'the cup of tea given...to a neighbour.'

Later that morning we found ourselves in front of a microphone, being questioned in a conversational way about our decision. We shared with those sitting before us the way God had planned and engineered everything, eventually changing our feelings so that now we longed to join the Christians in our own locality. I was able to state truthfully that the Lord had given me a love for the people I was going amongst, nothing to do with my own capacity to love, for I did not even know them but *His* love in my heart for our new family. Bruce explained,

'We don't want to leave you, but we know we must go — and we can't wait to get there!'

It was wonderful to have John's blessing on our mission, but sad to say goodbyes afterwards over coffee. We sensed doubtful reactions from some who questioned our wisdom:

'Don't you know West Wycombe is steeped in the occult?'

'You know there's a witches' coven there' warned a social worker who had experience of treating teenagers disturbed by involvement with local Satanist circles.

'Of course they have connections with Freemasonry,' chimed in a third.

'Yes, we know. The Lord has been warning us to claim His victory,' we asserted.

'You'll regret it!' from one of little faith.

'It makes no difference,' we pleaded, 'if the Lord tells you to go, you have to go!'

It was only later, at home, when all the clamour had died down that Bruce and I admitted to a feeling in our hearts of 'What *have* we done?!'

What a joy to be told next morning in Matthew 25:23:

'Well done, good and faithful servant.'

* * * * *

Chapter 11
Candles

November 1980

'So many candles…I am easily distracted by them…borne aloft by acolytes…to and fro…bobbing up and down. Now a procession bearing gifts…a server moves forward to assist the priest (I had never used *that* word before), dressed in elaborate and colourful robes…formality and ritual…I hope they don't use incense…it makes me cough.'

I sat in a daze, like a new girl at school, trying to concentrate on the A.S.B. service. It should have been familiar to me, but confused thoughts whirled through my brain; it all seemed strange and unreal.

St. Lawrence's was like no other church I had seen before. We were seated in an 'Egyptian Hall',[*1] mock porphyry pillars standing sentinel on the perimeter, petrified grapes and flowers encrusting the walls, canopied by a ceiling heavily decorated with daisies in geometric patterns. Inlaid, in the centre of the marble floor, was a design like the sun, hopefully to the glory of the Sun of Righteousness (Malachi 4:2 RSV) and not of the Temple of the Sun[*2] at Palmyra on which the nave was modelled.

[*1] A description the diarist, Mrs. Libby Powys, used on her visit to the church in 1775 shortly after its renovation by Sir Francis.

[*2] Or Temple of Bel.

Standing over this motif was a unique font: a decorated wooden pole with a carved snake curling its way up towards the doves drinking at the top. With a shock of reality, it spoke to me of the ever-present evil prowling and menacing near those who drink the 'waters of life'. But, praise the Lord, the doves are safe; this snake is destined never to overcome them!

St. Andrew's Day had arrived at last (yes, God does have a sense of humour!) and how significant that it was Advent Sunday too, with its promise of things to come. I listened carefully to the lessons: Isaiah 52 foretold that 'a messenger is coming', whilst the reading from Thessalonians reminded us to encourage one another in faith, love and hope. I knew God was with us.

I felt conspicuous, sitting there with the family on one of the front pews, 'in the round', especially when we missed the first 'shift' at the Communion rail through not knowing the routine. At the end of the service we were publically welcomed by the Vicar and many people came up to us to say 'Hello!' We felt their warmth and acceptance, and knew that love would be returned.

On being properly introduced to Lorna, I realised I had come face to face with the spiritual leader of the West Wycombe ladies — the very hub of the wheel. By first appearances she was an unusual mixture of shyness and confidence. I have come to respect her wisdom and calming influence.

At close hand, I soon realised the impact that Diana's illness was having on the village. Many had hoped that after her mastectomy all would be well again, but hopes tottered when she re-entered hospital to have her ovaries removed. People spoke in hushed whispers about her cancer, and asked me, 'Do you know about Diana?' They were surprised when I said I did, as if it were their own secret, but little is secret in West Wycombe.

Of course, Diana was not down-hearted. Her energy could not be squashed and she gaily assured everyone who enquired, that her prayers for healing would be answered, and woe betide anyone who disagreed!

*****

I took a further step of initiation when I attended an open meeting of the Parochial Church Council, early in December. Feeling the need to be 'put in the picture', as fully as possible, regarding our new church, I had decided to go along, especially since the topic 'Children in Church' would be on the agenda. I had never been to a PCC meeting before in my life and had no idea of the formalities or procedures.

It was also my first visit inside our Church Room in the High Street, a 15th Century building once used as a monastery, and later as a court house, complete with lock-up. It is a dark and musty room, with two unobliging wooden pillars in the middle of it. Sitting there in the meeting I found that they obscured my view of some of the members, and I had to crane my neck from side to side to see who was speaking.

Since the topics for discussion were most important ones, I was disappointed to discover that there were only nine people present. It was proposed that our church should participate in a scheme known as 'Partners in Mission', which would involve a long, hard look at the state of the church in Buckinghamshire, conducted by invited Christian leaders from all over the world. I was pleased when the motion was carried, as I sensed it would be an exciting project.

The agenda moved on through other topics, until I was jolted out of my reverie by the words…'so we may as well close the Sunday School and keep the children in for the whole service.' I gasped and inwardly exclaimed, 'No, No!' Outwardly, I held on to my composure and waited for my chance to intervene.

When it came, I tried, hesitantly, to explain how the Lord

had told me to come and help with the children, and how Diana and Lorna saw this as an answer to their prayer. I explained that I was a qualified teacher, although I had not taken Sunday School for about twenty years. I said that I would do my best if they would give me a chance. I did not realise at the time that it was out of order for me to butt in like that. The meeting kindly overlooked my ignorance and accepted my offer. Later, I wrote in my diary:

> 'Told them the Lord had directed me to the Sunday School. Felt, afterwards, I had maybe been too bold. Why should I be so bold?'

However, it was too late to regret lack of niceties. The job was in my lap and I would have to make the best of it. It was up to the Lord to lead me, as I had no idea what I would teach. I prayed a great deal about it and eventually managed to write down some aims that I hoped to carry out:

1. To bring the children into a close relationship with the Living Lord:
2. To increase their interest, excitement and curiosity about the Christian life, i.e. create a hunger.
3. Improve family relationships.

These three by means of: worship, prayer, listening, obedience and action, these never being an end in themselves, but a means to an end, i.e. a way to the Lord.

I felt excited about my new task, and even more so, when on the day that I was due to meet Lorna and the Vicar for the actual handing over of the Sunday School roll, with ensuing discussion, my morning scripture read:

'Feed my lambs.'   (John 21:15 RSV)

* * * * *

We discovered that there were two mid-week groups, meeting one in the afternoon, and one in the evening. Bruce and I decided to attend one each, and so it was that I found myself sitting one afternoon in Lorna's front room with a few core Christians, being inspired by a David Pawson tape on 'Revelation'. Inevitably the discussion turned to the latest events in our church, and someone mentioned prayer.

Diana commented 'I've heard it said that our church needs to be prayed in.'

I felt convinced that this was my cue to share something the Lord had shown me. I spoke up. 'For some time now, I've had on my mind a picture of myself, kneeling in prayer in St. Lawrence's — not in the regular Sunday service, but in an empty church. Would anyone be willing to come up to the church with me to pray for renewal?'

Lorna and Diana immediately agreed, and a couple of days later on a Thursday morning we began what was to become our regular pilgrimage up the hill.

It was warm work climbing West Wycombe Hill, as we left the lane and picked our way over tussocky grass to the old eastern gate of the grave-yard. We arrived a little out of breath and unlocked the huge red door of the church.

As we entered the nave, our voices fell to a whisper. It seemed strange to be in this awesome building on our own. It was rather eerie and we were glad of each other's company. We sidled into a pew and knelt down.

I was aware of my body being held in the exact position that I had visualised in my mind. A tremendous sense of 'rightness' swept through me and I was filled with peace. For the first time, we three prayed together, pleading with God to save and heal, to build and renew our church. Perhaps my companions did not feel it so 'right' — after all, they had become used to praying together as prayer-partners, and I was an outsider. If they did find it odd, they were kind enough not to say so.

Every Thursday we continued to trek up to St. Lawrence's, though Diana sometimes begged to be excused through ill-health. My new friends soon acquainted me with the work, so far, of the Holy Spirit in their midst. It was very exciting to hear that two or three of them had experienced the Baptism of the Spirit, and received the gift of tongues, whilst praying together in the smaller church of St. Paul's in the village. (We have two buildings to maintain!).

'Do you speak in tongues?' Diana asked me bluntly.

'No, I don't,' I said, to her surprise, and added, defensively, 'I don't think tongues is a compulsory sign of the Baptism in the Spirit.'

It's strange how we can say and mean one thing, whilst feeling quite differently in our hearts! It was my constant prayer to receive the gift, for I now knew that God gives this prayer language so that we may pray according to the Spirit when we have no idea of God's will in a certain situation. Here I was in a 'foreign' church, ignorant of its real condition and of its people, yet I had a commission to pray. 'I must have that gift of tongues Lord!'

At home, in private, I would try and believe that I had received it and would move my lips and make a sound from my throat, hoping that something would sound like a language, but it never did. Probably my attitude was wrong, but God was working on it!

One day, not long afterwards, two women came to my door. They were Jehovah's Witnesses. For once, I was not in a hurry, and although not keen to engage in a lengthy discussion, I did stop and have a few words with them. I felt it important to tell them of the orthodox Christian teaching on the Trinity, which J.W.'s disagree with. They, in turn, tried to put over their point of view. They were so obviously way off track that my heart went out to them, and I longed for them to see the truth.

In desperation, I said, 'Look, can I pray for you, that you will know God's truth? What is your name?'

'Yes, please do; my name's Joan,' came the earnest reply.

I shut the door as hastily as I could without wanting to

appear rude and dashed back to the kitchen. I clung on to the cooker, overcome by the urgency to pray there and then — but how, in what way? My mouth worked more quickly than my intellect and words rushed out 'Abba, abba...'

I do not know what followed, but a torrent of prayer poured out in an unknown tongue. God had answered my prayer when I really felt the need for it and I didn't care what it sounded like. I felt exhausted but exhilarated when I finally stopped. I realised that this was a further turning point in my life. The Lord had further equipped me for his work. Could it possibly be a reward for obedience too?

On thinking over the situation I became alarmed. Should I, or should I not, tell Bruce about my new gift? He had been rather low again. The problems at work were no nearer to being solved, and although it was great to have a three-day weekend, we were struggling to pay the bills. Despondency got the better of him once more. He confided to me that he feared going astray again.

'What's brought on this mood?' I asked.

'Well, the welcome has worn off. Nothing has happened and we've been at St. Lawrence for six weeks now!'

It was difficult for me not to laugh with incredulity. Had he really expected renewal so soon?! I reminded him that our commission was to love and to pray. Perfect love was needed. We just had to persist.

Bruce seemed a little calmer after our talk, though he did not like me apparently knowing the answers, even if he had asked for them. On reflection, I decided not to tell Bruce just yet about my new tongue, but prayed that God would similarly bless him so that he would not feel neglected. It was hard to keep it a secret, but I used it as much as I could in private prayer.

I was most anxious about my husband, and constantly prayed that he would find inner peace and contentment. I would often bubble over with thoughts that had come to me during the day, in either a prayer group or meditation, but Bruce showed no sign of being tuned in. Perhaps his reception was clouded by anxieties and fears about his job and worries about his responsibility for the family.

At one of the last Lydia meetings I attended at St. Andrew's, (I resisted letting that go for a few more weeks), we each had a marvellous sense of Jesus sitting amongst us, telling us that he loved us. We spent two hours in pure worship that day, feeling so close to the Lord, as if at His feet. I was filled with amazement and trepidation when, for the first time I was given a prophecy, but in that loving atmosphere I was able to speak out the Lord's words:

> 'I want you to depend entirely on Me. Have no other life separate from Me. You will find joy in this obedience.'

I thanked the Lord for using me to speak out to others, but I knew the words were for me too. We must be sure to do nothing separate from God, for He is interested in every, yes, every, aspect of our lives and wants to be Lord of each part.

I remembered the day I had given my life totally to the Lord. I was waiting at a bus-stop in Singapore. In a moment of revelation it became clear to me that giving one's life to God does not necessarily mean becoming a mousey missionary in Mozambique, (a conviction I had previously held). If I trusted God enough I would realise that He planned only fulfilment and the abundant life for me, and by His power would bring it to pass if I let Him, because He loved me. If indeed He did send me to Africa one day, He would first have given me the desire to go.

I wanted to share my prophecy with Bruce, for I was sure it would help to resolve his difficulties which he blamed on his lack of money. Why could he not see that putting everything in God's hands would help? In spite of, or because of, a blank response to my fruitless attempts to help him, I continued to pray, and the Lord encouraged me with words from Anne White's 'Dayspring' again, such as:

> 'I now speak the word of authority for your loved one. Believe that his healing is taking place'

and on another day:
'Let me banish this anxiety over your loved one.
You cannot intercede with faith when you are
consumed with fear'.

*****

I was so glad that the Lord had brought us to St. Lawrence's
for the Partners in Mission (P.I.M.) year, for it was like the
first glimmer of spring for our church — a time for growth
to begin, the first tentative shoots appearing, well before the
blossoming, but with definite signs of hope. It had arisen out
of a general desire for a 'taking-stock' of ourselves, a
self-examination of our church. Maybe there was a
conscious need for a spring-cleaning job, a putting of our
house in order, of cleaning the skeletons out of the
cupboards.'

Perhaps nobody knew what to expect or what would
result, or if indeed there would *be* any results at all. Perhaps
there was a little anxiety in some quarters, even fear, about
what would be expected, or revealed. So it took a step of
faith to commit ourselves, as a church, to the project. In
spite of many doubts and forebodings, ('They'll never
come...') seven house groups were set up to tackle the six
week study course set by the diocese.

Some of the groups undertook 'Rafts and Trawlers', a
course designed to investigate whether your church is
merely keeping afloat, or is actually in the business of
'fishing for men'. Bruce and I led a group studying 'Barriers
and Bridges', concerning personal relationships with God
and other people. The vicar and church wardens were
expected to take a critical look at the use of time, buildings,
materials, money and general administration of the church.

It is very difficult to know and assess oneself, although it
maybe much easier to criticise one's church! It is
undoubtedly difficult to bare one's soul and discuss one's
inner most thoughts and feelings with other people, when

one has never done so before. Many of us found discussion in groups embarrassing, and yet, amidst the resistance, the Lord was opening people's minds to greater possibilities in the life of our church.

The 'Partners' arrived and became absorbed into all areas of the county. Our own advisor and assessor, Pavel Javornicky, was a pastor from Czechoslovakia. He must have known far more about hardship and perseverance than we did, and his presence in the project made us realise how blessed we are, in Britian, to enjoy religious freedom.

Some of us were inclined to feel complacent, that all was well here, and no one need suffer persecution but could quietly jog along unchallenged, uncommitted, not allowing our religion to hinder the normal course of our lives. 'Why change ourselves or our church? We're doing very nicely thank you, and as for outreach — well, we've done our bit. We invited the ailing Methodists to join us. It's not our fault if they didn't want to!' As one would expect, where the power of the Holy Spirit had not been welcomed in, there was strong reluctance to sharing the faith with others, through fear, and lack of special ability with words.

At the time of P.I.M. we could not see the wood for the trees and now and again we wondered 'What is the point?' However, there were decisions stemming from that mission that were to have far-reaching effects and are still reflected in our attitude today. Of the many suggestions that were offered, only a small percentage were followed through. Of those, the majority were superficial, but they did succeed in creating a greater sense of community.

This was a springboard for involving more people in the life of the church, and our number of permanent house-groups grew from two to five, including a teenagers' club, Ikthus. The newly-born Prayer-Chain has grown steadily in spite of a general confession that prayer does not come easily.

A few people were challenged, by Pavel's commitment to us, to pray all the more fervently for the renewing power of

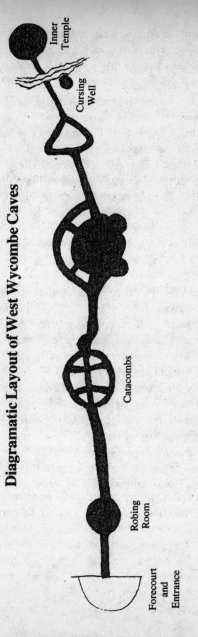

Diagramatic Layout of West Wycombe Caves

Inner Temple

Cursing Well

Catacombs

Robing Room

Forecourt and Entrance

117

the Holy Spirit to light up our lives, to fill God's people with real love for Him and to bring us out of our complacency into the Spirit-filled life. The three of us who prayed together in the church on Thursdays became keenly aware of our need for repentance, both individually and as a body, and a need for a deep cleansing of the whole area from real or imagined spirits of evil that hung over us like a mist.

We were unhappy with the way our church condoned Freemasonry. The St. Lawrence Lodge was invited annually to our Patronal Festival and laid on refreshments afterwards for our congregation. It was thought that the Lodge made a generous donation, though it was never proved. According to John Lawrence,[3] Freemasonry 'offers a way to God through knowledge and adherance to a moral code', and 'innoculates countless men against a need for Christ'.

We also felt the danger of association with the occult. It is popular knowledge that in the mid-eighteenth century the 'Brotherhood of St. Francis of Wycombe' (the Hell Fire Club) moved their headquarters from Medmenham Abbey to West Wycombe caves,[4] after these had been excavated by the baronet to provide both chalk for the new main road, and work for many villagers who were unemployed due to a succession of poor harvests. A Pedestal was erected at the threshold of the village to mark the road's completion. Although much of the written evidence has now been burned and little contemporary proof of the Club's evil activities exists, magazines and newspapers of that day are known to have reported wild rites and mock religious services, arousing curiosity far and wide.

What was the reason for such an elaborate system of

[3] Freemasonry: a Way of Salvation — J. Lawrence.

[4] Mrs. Powys's diary states that according to local tradition the Hell Fire Club occasionally met in the caves.

tunnels and chambers, bearing names such as Robing Room, Banqueting Hall and Inner Temple? The design is thought to have a connection with the Eleusinian Mysteries of ancient Greece. These were secret rites for the appeasement of the agrarian goddess, Ceres. According to mythology, she came to Eleusis to mourn for her daughter lost in the Underworld. While she mourned, the earth was barren. A bargain was struck whereby Persephone was rescued, but in return must spend part of each year as Hades' wife. She was also known as 'the Nymph of the R. Styx'. The Eleusinian sanctuary was cut into the flank of a hill, representing the entrance to the Underworld.

The caves might well have been used for the immoral revelry in which the Club indulged and even for the black magic in which 'St.' Francis had a 'passionate interest'.[*5]

Even if the 'Monks' merely dabbled in it in 'a light-hearted way' as has been suggested, the door would have been opened for the devil to put his toe in.

I suspect the club was also influenced by Rosicrucianism, an occult movement that was rife in the eighteenth century. It is probable that Sir Francis, would have made its acquaintance, if not at home, then on the continent where he travelled widely. The unusual lamp which once lit the Banqueting Hall featured doves and a serpent with its tail in its mouth — a Rosicrucian emblem, as was a daisy with twenty-two petals. Strange that there is a large XXII carved into the chalk wall of the underground passage! So closely linked with this cult were the Freemasons that the third degree of Rosicrucianism was considered qualification enough to enter Masonry, whilst the eighteenth degree of the latter secret society was modelled on Rosicrucian rites and beliefs.

In 1954, when Sir John Dashwood ordered repair work to the caves, miners reported feeling a draught of fresh air

---

[*5] Donald McCormick: 'The Hell Fire Club.'

from a passage reputed to connect with the church. Many believe*⁶ that the huge golden ball, twenty feet in diameter that perches above the tower, was the meeting place for Sir Francis' drinking parties, 'divine milk punch' being the order of the day; for what else would the seating inside it be?

Others claim there was no more than a 'topping-out' ceremony when Sir Francis completed his renovation of the church in 1763. Even so, one wonders at his intentions, since, from his youth he had detested the Catholic church, having suffered a strictly religious tutor, and had actively ridiculed Christian ritual.*⁷ He was said to have an implacable hatred of Popery, 'Anglican white magic, and evangelistic emotionalism',*⁸ but was much preoccupied with pagan rites.*⁹ Could it be that his designs for the new St. Lawrence's were born out of rebellion against both Papist and Puritan ideas.*⁸ One is also led to wonder why he crowned the church-tower with anything but a cross. The church of St. Lorenzo, in Florence, with a tower strikingly similar to that of St. Lawrence, is capped with only a small golden ball, but with a large cross above it.

*⁶ From the writings of John Wilkes M.P., member of the Hell Fire Club.

*⁷ Sir Francis Dashwood: 'The Dashwoods of West Wycombe' (1987) pp 26, 36, 51.

*⁸ 'The Hell-Fire Club' — D. McCormick pp 45-48, 62.

*⁹ B.J. Bailey: 'View of the Chilterns' pp 47, 51, 54.

St. Lorenzo's Basilica in Florence.

How much was this aura of evil affecting life in the village today? How much was publicity for profit's sake perpetuating the notion that the village was an occult site. Such an atmosphere would be likely to attract those actively engaged in witchcraft today.

We began to pray earnestly for purity and holiness.

One beautiful Thursday morning in early autumn, I met Lorna at the church for our prayer-time as usual. Since the cleaners had already arrived and were busily sweeping and shaking out hassocks, we found a bench in the churchyard and sat down. What peace we found there, and assurance once again of being in 'the right place'. We sat in silence for a while, asking the Lord to direct our thoughts. I was surprised how many sounds there were - country noises of birds, and branches crackling in the breeze. When I listened really carefully, I could even hear the leaves fall.

We both knew that God was showing us a parable: speaking to us of the falling and dying that must come before the spring, the laying down and making bare, before the blossoming. Lorna was given three words during the silence.

LISTEN — WAIT — TEACH

We puzzled over the unexpected order of the words. We would have preferred to teach and then wait for results. It set us pondering. During our prayers we felt led to hand everything over into the Lord's hands — ourselves, our church, the vicar, the congregation, our hopes and dreams, our worries and responsibilities.

What a relief! We knew it was all in good hands. We would wait!

Chapter 12
Bright Light

February 1982

Our Prayer and Praise group began with just four people. The other two were our Christian neighbours, John and Brenda Fisher. It was cold in St. Paul's in February, but with the help of their electric fire which they brought with them, and a set of 'Songs of Victory' which they had donated to our church, our hearts glowed warmly as we experienced the wonderful peace and freedom God gives us in response to our praise. God had commanded us 'to pray as if to open prison doors' (29.10.80). What was it that opened Paul's and Silas' prison? PRAISE (Acts 16:25).

We met every week, and sometimes one or two from the village would join us. Our friendship with the Fishers led us into many a meaty discussion, some of which were unsettling, as they should be if they are pin-pointing our weaknesses of faith or conviction. It was a time of thinking deeply and dealing with the 'woolly' areas of our Christianity. Bruce was often pulled in two opposing directions, as he continued to worry over work and money, and sometimes did not join us in our praise sessions.

He swung back and forth like a pendulum, one day seething with rebellion against God, and me, and nonchalantly claiming he had not prayed for a week — a few days later confiding that whilst sitting in church he had recommitted his life to the Lord! I did not know what to think with so many changes of mood. One morning over breakfast I said,

'Last night, just before I went to sleep, I saw a very bright dazzling light, even though I had my eyes shut'.

'That's amazing,' said Bruce. 'I saw a bright light too, and Jesus was standing in it!'

The position at work was so fragile that Bruce was not even sure that he would receive the next pay packet. Eventually, in spite of the pull of loyalty to the firm, Bruce began to look for 'Situations Vacant'. There were not many available, but he wrote for an interview with a local firm.

I prayed desperately. 'Lord, Bruce thinks a job with plenty of money will be the answer to his problem. I pray that you will give him what he wants, so that he may learn that it is not the whole solution'. We should be careful what we pray, for we usually get what we ask for. I have often wondered since whether or not that was a wise prayer, for the answer has led to more difficulties and I feel partly responsible.

At the same time that this turmoil was raging, another, most surprising development had occurred. In several ways, Bruce had become aware of the alleged benefits of tithing one's money, that is, the biblical concept of giving one-tenth of one's income to God's use. I had dropped a few comments about 'other people who tithe', but did not expect Bruce to be enchanted with the idea. By coincidence, the Fishers had mentioned it in Bruce's hearing, too.

Despite all our difficulties, in one of Bruce's more uplifted moments, he decided to follow suit. I could hardly believe it, but was overjoyed and prayed in faith that God would honour this step of obedience. He did, of course, and thankfully it was soon after that Bruce had news of his new job, offering plenty of work and a substantial increase in salary.

* * * * *

'I know what you are doing; I know that you have the reputation of being alive, even though you are dead! So wake up, and strengthen what you still have before it dies completely. For I find that what you have done is not yet perfect in the sight of my God. Remember then, what you were taught and what you heard; obey it and turn from your sins. If you do not wake up I will come upon you like a thief and you will not even know the time when I will come'. (Revelation 3:1-3 GNB)

I was cut to the quick — stunned as though from a slap on the face. 'O Lord,' I prayed, on that bleak February morning, 'surely not! Am I really dead? Is that what you think of me?'

What had begun as a routine quiet-time with the Lord, reading through the early chapters of Revelation at a rather shallow level, had become a personal attack. How awful! 'Is this really true? Have I been fooling myself? Does God require an act of deep repentance from me?' I had to know.

Fortunately, that same day two good Christian friends were due to come round for an hour's Bible Meditation with me. They were both from other churches. Before we could begin I had to ask them to weigh up this penetrating reading for me.

'Is it for me?' I pleaded. 'Please tell me truthfully.'

'The Holy Spirit never harshly accuses. He is the still small voice,' soothed Barbara.

'No,' chimed in Brenda, 'it's a prophetic warning for your church. I know it is.' The words stayed on her mind, and the next day she handed me a scrap of paper. 'I looked up Revelation 3:1-5 in my commentary, and then the Lord gave me this prophecy for your church.'

Her uneven scrawl was difficult to read, but the message came out strong and clear.

'Be alert, watching and praying. The fruit of the Spirit exists in your church, but very feebly. Remember what you have received and heard.

125

Hold fast — for many church members find more pleasure in the things of the world than in a prayer-meeting, or the things of the Spirit. The devil is not asleep, but very much alive and on the job, seeking whom he can devour. Your church has lost its zeal and become dead. It must be strengthened immediately.'

I knew I must pass on this message to those who would pray and to the leadership. I prayed that these words would be like the two-edged sword of the Spirit (Ephesians 6:17) and pierce to the exact spot where it was required to do its work (Hebrews 4:12 GNB).

'The word of God is alive and active, sharper than any double-edged sword. It cuts all the way through to where soul and spirit meet, to where joints and marrow come together.'

A couple of days later I was led again to read Revelation, only this time in chapter two. My eyes were immediately drawn to the words;

'This is the message from the one who has the sharp two-edged sword...'

('Yes, Lord', I replied, and continued to read.)

'...I know where you live, there where Satan has his throne...'

('O Lord, is it really true?')

'...You are true to me and did not abandon your faith in me even during the time when Antipas my faithful witness was killed.' (Revelation 2:13 GNB)

Now what did that mean? Who had been killed? I knew of no-one in the past to fit that description. Could it mean Diana? I had an uncomfortable feeling that it was a prophecy, written in the 'prophetic past' tense. Diana had recently confided in the Tuesday group that once, in her youth, and consumed with fervent commitment to the Lord, she had selflessly prayed that she would die young, and in her death be a witness for God.

Such a prayer is far more easily made in one's idealistic

126

youth, unencumbered with responsibilities. Fulfilling as it is to have our family around us, it does make single-minded determination for the Lord much more difficult. We cannot trifle with God; his timing is perfect. He chooses the exact times in our lives when we are ready to make commitments to him.

The message to the church at Pergamum (Revelation 2:14) went on to warn that there were some among us falling into idolatry and immorality. We were turning away from God and giving our love to other things.

We must turn in repentance to God; we must love and serve him in the way he deserves — whole heartedly. In Old Testament times God showed in dramatic ways his intolerance of idolatry.

'Thou shalt have no other gods before me'

(Exodus 20:3 KJV)

came the command again and again, but still today we put other considerations before God's wishes. What are our idols? Work, sport, television, horoscopes, cars, education, even family, are put first on our list of priorities.

'I cannot go to church because I have visitors coming', it is reasoned. Surely we can tell our relatives that God comes first with us!

'I cannot keep a quiet-time with God for prayer and Bible-reading because I'm *so* busy!' But did we ask God to arrange our day so as to make the best use of our time?

Even in the church, any scheme or institution that lines our pockets, or makes a profit, is deemed acceptable, no matter whether or not it complies with God's laws of purity, holiness and love. Financial considerations count as more important than God's laws. The thousands of pounds that local Freemasons have donated to charity, seemed to render them respectable enough for publicity in our church magazine. (This was by way of explanation about why a body of unknown men descend annually on our church for its patronal festival.)

The 'immorality' (v.14) spoke to me of betrayal and

127

abandonment of the one who loves us, namely God. Have we betrayed Jesus by departing from his gospel of repentance and salvation through the cross? Have we been unfaithful to him by looking for more delectable 'gospels', because they seem easier or more acceptable to the masses? More acceptable? The masses have turned away from the Lord and their hearts have become cold.

> *'So repent. If you don't I will come to you soon and fight against those people with the sword that comes out of my mouth'.* (v.16 GNB)

There is no virtue in pointing the finger — we all share in the corporate sin of our church. There is no alternative to the 'narrow gate', no way so perfect or satisfying as the way through the refiner's fire.

> *'To those who win the victory I will give some of the hidden manna'* (v.17 GNB)

Praise God that he keeps his promises!

Yes, God was beaming the light of understanding into our midst, showing us more clearly our dark areas, defining what he requires of us. If he intended us to do more than pray about these things, then we failed miserably. As a prophetic voice to our church, we were weak and feeble, perhaps because our tentative attempts fell on deaf ears. However, we continued to pray.

*****

A few responded to the light in positive ways. In spite of setbacks, not least being Diana's deteriorating condition, we had much for which to 'Praise the Lord'. My next-door neighbour became a Christian. It happened during one of our outreach coffee evenings which we had continued to hold since the Barry Kissel Mission. Shena told me that in 1977, God had indicated that she would go on a five-year journey to find the truth. Now she had found it! What rejoicing! It was a delight for me to see my friend grow as a new child of God, being broken, melted, remoulded and

128

used in his service. She joined us in the Prayer and Praise meetings and blessed us by the way she listened to God's voice.

She, and a couple of other ladies were eventually baptised in the Spirit and received the gift of tongues. It was a great blessing for them, but sad that in every case it happened outside the bosom of the church family. It had not been encouraged or witnessed by the main body of believers in St. Lawrence's.

Coming home from a weekend Youth Leaders' Course with the Good News Crusade, where one of our Ikthus leaders had been similarly blessed, I encouraged Bruce to attend a Praise and Renewal meeting at a well-known church in Hounslow.

'May it bless you as much as this weekend has blessed me', I said, as I waved him off. While he was out I prayed again that Bruce would receive God's gift of tongues. When he returned I could see from his face, before he said a word, that my prayer had been answered. Our spirits were lifted as we explored this new dimension of praise together.

I was also blessed through my Seekers Group (Sunday School) which was now flourishing. As I leaned on the Lord for guidance and encouragement in this field, I learned a great deal and enjoyed the work of planting seeds, seeing them grow before my very eyes.

By the summer, it was impossible for Diana to walk up to the church with us for prayer, so our trio moved to her garden, or living-room (and later, her bedroom). This more convenient rendezvous attracted more pray-ers and we grew to half-a-dozen. The suggestion that we become a 'Lydia Group' was readily accepted and we began to learn together the delights of waiting on the Lord, to hear his directions and to pray according to His will.

At our very first 'Lydia-type' meeting, we prayed for the Argentinians to surrender, in the Falklands war. That same evening we learnt from the six o'clock news that this had indeed happened, due to the tireless work of a lady-doctor,

129

negotiating peace throughout that afternoon eight thousand miles away. We felt God's seal of approval on our deeper dependence on him.

From the very beginning I kept a written record of the words of promise and encouragement that the Lord gave us, also his warnings and commands. We were given continual words of assurance that the Lord was with us, loving us, pruning us, building us up.

'Do not worry. Do not fear.
Trust me.
I will make you a sure foundation stone'.

Sometimes the message was hard to receive, but, uplifted in love we bravely shared it in the group and obediently prayed it through. He gave us a picture of the Gardener's Hand, cutting off useless branches and burning them, leaving the fruitful ones. With this came the command, 'Prune yourselves, or God will do it.'

A constant theme was 'repentance', with a penetrating warning —

'Change or decay.'
'You are like Mary's alabaster jar. You must be broken open before the beautiful perfume is able to escape.'
'Your fields have been ploughed up but there is no seed growing because the birds have come and eaten it up.'

We knew, from the parable of the Sower (Mark 4:14-15) that the seed was the Word of God, and the birds were symbolic of the devil.

'TELL THEM', said the Lord, again and again.

We prayed desperately for obedient hearts that we may go into action with the strength and power of the Holy Spirit. We prayed for wisdom to know how to proceed; for repentance and new life for our church, that we may be a praising people. The Lord fuelled our prayers with promises and exhortations:

*'The Cedars of Lebanon are crushed by evil, but
new life will rise up out of it.'*
*'The Lord, thy God in the midst of thee is mighty.
He will save.'*   (Zephaniah 3:17 KJV)
'Thy people shall be my people.'

However, the most dramatic signs of God's purpose
among us have been the pictures he has formed in our
minds, keeping the vision before us. He showed us a
fountain in St. Lawrence's with all the people sitting in it
enjoying the water splashing over them.

Many pictures featured light, such as the lighthouse
shining out over a choppy sea with dark clouds looming, or
shafts of light shining through a dense wood.

*'The light shines in the darkness, and the darkness
has never put it out'*   (John 1:5 GNB)

One of our earliest pictures showed us three people, the
vicar, Diana, and a child, standing in the light, but sadly
their faces were turned away from it. Perhaps these three
were symbolic of the leadership, the laity and the young
people.

In spite of the breakthrough that God was making into our
lives, we often found it difficult to actually start praying; it
was far more tempting to sit and talk. We progressed in a
rather erratic way, with many ups and downs, perhaps
reflecting Diana's condition in ours. She was sometimes in
agony with pain, sometimes just numb, at other times,
riding her bicycle all the way from Bledlow Ridge. When
she was low the whole village was low.

Her mood was one of enthusiasm as we gathered in the
Church Room in September to reorganise the various house
groups and to muster more support for them. Diana gaily
invited our Prayer and Praise group to amalgamate with the
Tuesday Group for she said that several would like to
participate in both activities.

This proved to be the beginning of a year of struggle
within this group to submit our wills to the Lordship of
Christ in worship and prayer. God continued to speak to us

of pruning out our self-centred desires and feelings, but there was too much rebellion in us. Our praise was shallow. We were like trees with many leaves but no fruit. Our roots needed to grow more deeply into the Rock. It was a difficult time, like going into a long labour before giving birth. At times there was a love/hate relationship within the group as we grappled with beliefs and inhibitions. No doubt we hindered God's work through our disobedience, but the Lord, ever loving and merciful kept promising:

'Though the vision tarry — it will surely come.'

*****

By the end of the year, we were hoping and praying that Diana would see Christmas and be able to enjoy it with her family. She saw it, of course, and well beyond, but it was harrowing to watch her staggering with a walking stick, her face so drawn and thin, her legs wasting away. She was a fighter; she would not give in. Even in her physical weakness, she was the strength of her family.

Diana never gave up loudly trusting in the Lord. Some of her friends mustered all the faith they could to keep on praying for healing. Others never expected her to survive and looked on helpless. Both Lorna and I secretly held in our hearts the niggling conviction that God had said 'No' to our pleas. So how were we to pray? Was it hypocritical to go on asking for healing? Did it show lack of faith or defeatism to hand her over the the Lord and stop praying? It was a frustrating time.

As I sat in my 'thinking chair' one morning, looking out of my bedroom window and over the tops of the trees to the hills in the west, I begged God to give me 'a word', to show me how to pray, or what to do. As I sat relaxed, but alert and absorbing God's presence, a picture of a page of my Bible came clearly into mind. It was Psalm 116. I found the page and began to read.

'I love the Lord because he hears me, he listens to my prayers. He listens to me every time I call to him.' (v.1-2 GNB)

(Thank you Lord for hearing me.)

'The danger of death was all around me, the horrors of the grave closed in on me. I was filled with fear and anxiety. Then I called to the Lord. I beg you, Lord, save me.' (v.3-4 GNB)

(This must surely be concerning Diana, I thought, as I read on),

'The Lord is merciful and good, our God is compassionate. The Lord protects the helpless. When I was in danger he saved me. Be confident my heart because the Lord has been good to me.'

(v.5-7 GNB)

That was so true. The Lord is compassionate and merciful. He does save us from danger. Now he was telling me to be confident, the reason coming surely in the next verse.

'The Lord saved me from death, he stopped my tears, and kept me from defeat. And so I walk in the presence of the Lord in the world of the living. I kept on believing even when I said, "I am completely crushed"; even when I was afraid and said "No one can be trusted".' (v.8-11 GNB)

Diana had indeed often wondered if she could trust the doctors, and here was a promise, surely, of a saving from death. With every promise comes a condition: I read on, searching for it. It was not hard to find, for the psalmist spoke of a promise made, of a wine-offering of thanksgiving that was due. (v.12-14)

'In the assembly of all your people, in the sanctuary of your Temple in Jerusalem, I will give you what I have promised.' (v.18-19 GNB)

'Well', I thought, 'I must tell Diana at once. All we have to do is find out what Diana has promised the Lord. Then she can give it to Him and all will be well'.

'Oh no,' countered Diana's voice at the other end of the phone, 'I haven't made any promise. That word's not for me — it's for you!'

I was incredulous. I went back to that psalm and read it all over again, relating it to myself. My thoughts flew back to those terrible days in Singapore before I really knew God's love for me, before He brought me from spiritual death into new life in Jesus. Indeed I had been filled with fear and anxiety (v.3) trying to live in my own strength. How I had begged God to save me (v.4) and how gently He stopped my tears and kept me from defeat. Well, what could I offer the Lord (v.12)? What had I promised? What was the wine-offering?

Only a matter of days lapsed before I began to write. I wrote in faith, relying on the Spirit to provide every word, believing it to be a part of God's plan for the renewal of His church. I began with the vision...

When Diana's death came it was unexpected. She had gone into hospital for another routine blood transfusion. She had wanted to be in church on Easter Day and yet again she kept her appointment. Only a week later, it was all over.

'Have you not fully recognised my victory over death?...You prayed and things did not happen as you wanted. This is the sting of death. Release this person to me' (from DAYSPRING).

*****

That same day, a Sunday, five children were born again, including my two sons. They professed a desire to turn around, stop pleasing themselves and start pleasing Jesus instead. They prayed individually and personally for Jesus to forgive their sin and to come into their hearts by His Holy Spirit. They each knew the real experience of the quickening flame of the Holy Spirit within them. What joy for them to know the excitement and reality of the Living Lord in their lives. The numbers peaked at twenty-one in the

Seekers Class that May, and a further eight children made a personal commitment to the Lord over the following months.

Through this we were inspired to go on praying for renewal for our whole congregation, with repentance and deeper commitment to Christ and an overflowing of the power and life of the Spirit in our church. God calls us to holiness and obedience. He calls us to open ourselves to his cleansing love, so that the channel is cleared for His Spirit to work among us.

'Clear the road of stones — make it good, says the Lord'. (Lydia 9.1.84)

God honours our obedience and answers our prayers. He Himself gives us the power to love Him and find joy in true worship.

> *'Let us celebrate our Passover then, not with bread having the old yeast of sin and wickedness, but with the bread that has no yeast, the bread of purity and truth'.* (1 Corinthians 5:8 GNB)

*****

Chapter 13
Spiritual Warfare —
The Battle is On

1982-84

To those who would question the reality of the devil, I would pose the following questions:

Why is it that, when circumstances are going well for God, evil rears its ugly head? Why is it that, when the people of God make progress in the work of the Kingdom of Heaven, they feel more keenly the attack of negative forces?

The answer is obvious. We are caught up in a spiritual battle, a battle for the world, between the Kingdom of Darkness, led by Satan, and the Kingdom of Light, over which our Lord Jesus Christ reigns supreme. The victory is assured, and has already been won when Jesus died on the Cross, defeating the power of sin and death over mankind, but the devil has not yet acknowledged his hopeless position. He constantly tries to fight back, snatching away the joy of the victorious life from as many as he can deceive.

For those who recognise this battle, God has provided the armour to ward off the attack of the enemy and the words to proclaim the victory by the authority of Jesus.

> *'I have been given all authority in heaven and earth'* (Matthew 28:18 GNB)

Jesus has handed authority to us who place ourselves under his authority. He declares:- *'What you prohibit on earth will be prohibited in heaven.'* (Matthew 18:18 GNB) That means we can, in Jesus name, prohibit evil powers from attacking us.

As we, in West Wycombe, saw a movement of the Holy Spirit working amongst us, so we began to feel the attack of the devil working against us. It was as though the occult powers from past and present that had taken over the land were making a desperate bid to fight us off.

'I feel a heavy weight bearing down upon this village, a huge, cold, hard mill-stone pressing down upon us, hindering renewal, stunting growth,' I mused. We were praying in the church again, Lorna and I, in the ancient chancel now.

Lorna told me, 'I had a strange dream. It was rather scary, but you and I, Ann, were going round the village casting out the devil!'

I was lost for words, but I am sure the expression on my face conveyed my alarm. How were we to know of such things, we who still had much to learn. We mentioned our fears, about the inherited presence of evil and the heavy weight, to our vicar who suggested we visit the Bishop's exorcist, an elderly monk living at Nashdom Abbey.

*****

As Bruce, Lorna and I sat down in the late Dom Robert's small sitting-room in the half-light of evening, the old man looked very ancient indeed.

'This is my idea of a sage', I thought.

His manner was very calm. He spoke softly and seemed anxious to avoid any hint of the sensational. He assured us that the church and caves had been prayed in, several years ago and all that was left to be done was to take care of the 'little devils', as he called them.

'Do not under-estimate the cleansing power of the Lord's Prayer, chanted very slowly and meaningfully', he advised.

He seemed tired and frail and we thought it tactful not to

137

outstay our welcome. We thanked him for his time and left. For me there was a sense of anti-climax, though the others seemed satisfied.

*****

For some years, I had made a point of never entering the village without praying for its protection in Jesus' name. Now I began to whisper the Lord's Prayer as I walked the quarter mile stretch from the Pedestal to the Post Office, and in various locations around West Wycombe, wherever I happened to be.

The Lord began to impress upon us, in Lydia, the need for spiritual discernment, a gift of the Holy Spirit (1 Corinthians 12), and for the spiritual armour to be appropriated. This is described in Ephesians Chapter 6 and consists of the helmet of faith, the breastplate of righteousness, the belt of truth, the sword of God's Word, the shield of faith, and the shoes of the Gospel of peace.

We were warned of the nearness of the spiritual dangers...

> *'For we fight not against flesh and blood, but against principalities, powers and the rulers of the darkness of the world and against spiritual wickedness in high places'* (Ephesians 6:12 KJV)

...especially to our families, and we began to learn about the protection that the blood of Jesus has won for us. 'There is nothing that makes the devil quake with fear more than the mention of the "Blood of Jesus",' came the advice of a wise Christian teacher Bruce and I met whilst on holiday in Scotland.

I welcomed a picture Shena had described to me of a shimmering blood-red cloak, beautiful and comforting, hanging in folds from head to toe. I began to use it as an aid to praying for the protection of our family, and others in a vulnerable position. I would pray, daily,

> 'O Lord, protect us by the blood of Jesus,'

and having prayed, I trusted Him to keep His Word, and found peace.

I was aware of the need to protect those children who had made a commitment to Jesus recently. Nevertheless, the Seekers Group was the first to fall into difficulties. By June the average attendance was reduced to ten, and it has continued to decrease ever since.

We warn our children that the stranger who offers them a lift in his car, or a confidence trickster at the door, will, more often than not, appear to be quite an ordinary and pleasant chap. It's not often that the 'baddies' are obviously wicked! So it is with the devil. He may work out his attacks even through one's own friends, one's own church, in what may seem to be a perfectly reasonable way.

A tremendous resistance set in from some factions to the new spiritual songs that we longed to introduce into the worship. Many beautiful songs have been inspired by the Holy Spirit during the past fifteen years, most of them incorporating words taken directly from Scripture, enabling the worshipper to express himself simply and joyfully. We came up against a barrier of criticism against them, the reasons difficult to fathom.

There was also resistance to any encouragement to 'open up' to the Lord, to respond to Him, to talk about Him. I suffered personal attack for the way I spoke about my faith, and was accused of preventing people from joining the church because of it! One of the sneakiest weapons the devil uses against our effectiveness is the spirit of rejection. I had a personal struggle with that one after a particularly cutting remark that I 'upset everybody'.

When we are at our lowest ebb, the Lord saves us. I remembered his promise to comfort me when falsely accused.* He said to us:

---

* Word from Anne White on 11.10.80.

139

'Raise up the cross in the High Street.'

'Fear not, rejoice and be glad.'

'Resist the devil and he will flee from you.'

(James 4:7 NIV)

'For this the Son came into the world — He was made manifest to destory the works of the Devil.'

'Pray for discernment. Pray that the Lord will come in the power of the Spirit and confirm, in faith, the Lord's victory!'

(extracts from Lydia notes)

*****

It was amazing how God was teaching me at every turn, through books I read, tapes or speakers I heard, about the urgency of spiritual warfare. My eyes were opened to the way the devil deceives and attacks our minds, or even our bodies. I was to learn to resist the devil so that he *would* flee from me, for he knows that in Jesus I have the victory in every situation, if only I will realise it and proclaim it.

I was made aware of the many demons which are able to attach themselves to us through certain weak or sinful places in our nature (rather like cracks and crevices in a castle wall) and if allowed to stay, begin to have such a hold over our lives that we cannot shake them off; they begin to rule our actions.

I was able to rid myself of two or three such demons of a very personal nature in my own life and knew for myself that I was truly free of them, for they have not had their way since. It would not be appropriate to go into details here of the specialised type of praying necessary for this type of cleansing, but such books as Michael Harper's 'Spiritual Warfare', or Frank Hammond's 'Pigs in the Parlour' are recommended reading prior to entering in to this activity. I merely mention it here to show that, with God's constant reminder to Lorna and myself to —

'Be ye therefore perfect — and seek holiness',

he was teaching us and providing the way to work out our salvation (Philippians 2:12), teaching us how to use the authority he had already provided through Jesus' death and victory on the cross. It was necessary to be clean vessels in order to carry out the Lord's work.

Bruce was much happier these days, enjoying his work in the consultancy office, and was indeed a churchwarden. Nevertheless, I was worried about a trace of rebelliousness, that occasionally surfaced, in his attitude to God. It would disappear for weeks, only to reappear suddenly as a set and alien look in his face that scared me, as though I was looking at a stranger.

It was just such an occurrance that led me to pray for him after we had attended a Spiritual Life Seminar in the town one evening. I sensed during the meeting that he was full of resistance, refusing to sing the lively new songs that he usually enjoyed so much, raising imaginary barriers between the speaker and himself, so that he would remain untouched by the message. We left early without chatting to our friends.

Once home I knew what I must do. There was no point in delaying any longer.

'Bruce, would you mind if I pray for you to be delivered from this rebellion? I think its a demon that's attacking you against your will. You may think it nonsense, or un-necessary, but there's no harm in praying.'

'All right, if you want to,' he grudgingly assented.

'Lord, I pray for the protection of the blood of Jesus over us, and I claim the authority of the name of Jesus.

I say to you, demon of rebelliousness, that in Jesus name you are bound and powerless. By the authority of His blood, you must come out — now. I tell you to go to the Lord Jesus Christ to be dealt with, and leave Bruce in peace.

'O Holy Spirit, come now and fill Bruce's heart afresh

with your Spirit, that he may be healed.'

I have never again seen that look of rebellion in Bruce's face.

*****

Even in the midst of adversity we see the ripples as the Spirit moves over the face of the waters (Genesis 1:2). God is at work amongst us, the Holy Spirit restraining the evil, even though human disobedience and failure to believe His Word hinder progress.

A vision of ourselves as an old clump of perennials, needing to be split in order to be invigorated, led to new leaders emerging from the Tuesday Fellowship for four new groups, including a second prayer-group and the long-awaited Men's Group — another answer to prayer. The original group continued, however, to meet fortnightly, for prayer, praise and bible-study.

The new ventures began with greater or lesser degrees of success but growth as before was sluggish. We would have hoped to have attracted larger numbers, considering the way the Sunday congregation had grown a little, but it takes time to gain people's interest and confidence, and for them to realise their need for Christian fellowship. Perhaps the term 'Bible-Study' is too academic; perhaps 'Adventures in God's Word' would be more accurate and inviting.

The Lord showed me, in my imagination, a picture of a race-course. He said that people are like horses — some are at the front pressing on urgently to the goal, others are slowing down, stopping to nibble the grass beside the track, yet others have turned around and are blithely ambling away in the wrong direction. Still, in our Lydia Group we were told:

'Use the opportunities you have to set people free. The church at Laodicea was imprisoned in ignorance. Pray for the preaching and feeding of the Word of God in your church. It is urgent — the harvest is ready.'

And then the lovely reassurance:

'I am the source of life — I will feed my sheep.'

That was a life-line to hang on to, since we leaders who were trying to feed the house-groups were, ourselves, under-nourished and untrained.

From time to time, the Lord would prophecy to us through our Prayer and Praise group, that is, when he could find an obedient soul willing to speak out his words. The most important of these came at our meeting on 25th October 1983.

In my preparation time before the meeting, I felt God was saying 'You must give an opportunity for people to ask for personal prayer tonight, even laying on of hands. Somebody needs special prayer'. I was shown, by the Holy Spirit gift of knowledge, who that person was. During the meeting I gave the invitation to ask for prayer two or three times in different ways, but there was no response to it. At least one person needed that prayer, for her body movements indicated it — the very person I had previously been shown — but she *would* not ask. Two others later privately and separately confirmed my convictions.

Before the end of the session I felt a strong prompting to speak out in tongues prophetically, although I rarely did this because I felt a resistance to it from some of the group. As soon as it had ceased, the interpretation was given by Shena:

'There is a short bright sword coming out of the mouth of Jesus which will pierce to the centre of our group'

I did not understand the prophecy fully at that moment, except to know that this was the Sword of the Spirit, the Word of God.

On reflection later, I turned to Revelation 2:16 again. After a warning about idolatry, God says:

'Now turn from your sins! If you don't, I will come

143

to you soon and fight against those people with the
sword that comes out of my mouth.'

A reluctance to praise God, to love and worship Him in the Body of Christ as He desires, a reluctance to turn to Him in prayer, caring more about the opinions of people, amounts to idolatry, surely, for in effect we are pushing God to one side and giving our own desires the place of paramount importance.

After a half-term break, we met for our Lydia meeting on the 7th November. The Lord cautioned us:

'Your church is not speaking to the 'stranger' in your midst.'

We interpreted that this referred to 'Jesus in our midst', that our prayer life was at fault, indeed prayer was, and is, the greatest area of resistance.

The Lord also said He wanted to bring peace and unity to this house (Luke 10:5) and that we must know one another better. He said:

'Pray for renewal for the whole church. One person's authority in the church is not the way it should be among you.'   (Luke 22:26 GNB)

We thought this referred to our whole congregation. Maybe it did, but with hind-sight it was obviously meant for our Prayer and Praise group too.

The meeting of Tuesday the 8th was not radically different from any of the others, except that there was a noticeable resistance to sensitive and spiritual prayer, and to the laying on of hands when Shena asked for prayer to receive the gift of knowledge.

As it turned out, that evening was to be the closing episode to a year's struggle to encourage and unite that group as an open and praising body. And yet, only one day earlier, the Lord had said,

'Peace and unity to your house!'

How could that be, for Jesus was a stranger in our midst, and our prayer life was at fault? I sensed an under-current of dissatisfaction which would have to be brought out into the open.

* * * * *

Two Lydia meetings took place before the next Prayer and Praise was due. On November 14th God told us to pray about our physical, moral and spiritual danger. He commanded us to testify and instruct others in the true faith. He also told us to bring, and do, what God requires:

'...*you are robbing me. Bring the whole tithe into the store house*' (Malachi 3:9&10 NIV)

'*Let us then , always offer praise to God as our sacrifice, through Jesus, which is the offering presented by lips that confess him as Lord.*' (Hebrews 13:15 GNB)

And from Ezekiel 17:10, he said:

'Yes it is planted, but will it live and grow?'

Applying this verse to our Prayer and Praise Group, it *had* been planted, but it would only grow and be blessed if people would obediently bring open hearts full of praise, and worship God as he requires. Worship means far more than the mere singing of songs, or the formation of a musical appreciation society. It cannot be learnt from a text book as an intellectual exercise.

We Lydias, few though we were, continued to cry out to God in prayer that he would prosper his renewing work in our church, bringing people to repentance and new life empowered by the Holy Spirit.

On 21st November the Lord reassured us:

'*Surely the arm of the Lord is not too short to save, nor his ear too dull to hear. But your iniquities have separated you from your God.*' (Isaiah 59:1 NIV)

'Pray that people respond to the Lord. The Lord is reigning — Praise Him.'

145

Just before leaving I said to Lorna, 'I hope all goes well tomorrow night. I think it will be an important turning point. *Something* is going to happen. The Tuesday Group will not be the same again.'

'Oh, by the way,' said Lorna, 'I shan't be there.'

'Oh no!' I gasped. 'I *need* your support.'

'Well, I've been asked to help at the Ikthus Group tomorrow and I agreed because I know I shall only lose my temper if I go with you. I feel so strongly about the whole issue. I have been reading "The Radical Christian" by Arthur Wallis in which he states so clearly that we must not compromise our faith. We must not commit the sin of tolerance where truth is at stake! It is not right that we should water down our prayer and worship to please those who don't even believe the Christian Gospel!'

Lorna was keen to discuss more of her findings in that inspired book, but I had to hurry home as it was getting late. I asked her to let me know the next day if she had any more helpful advice, before I went to the meeting. 'And I'm sure I can count on your prayers,' I said, as we parted.

I prayed spasmodically throughout the day on Tuesday, but did not feel anxious. I did ask the Lord that all should be done in love. Lorna rang and said, 'Can I see you?'

'I'll come at three for just half-an-hour,' I replied. Just as I was leaving the house I met Shena.

'I can't come tonight,' she called out.

'Oh no, not you too,' I moaned. I knew that Shena, too, felt a great need for that time of closeness with God.

'Just relax. Stay calm,' she soothed. 'Just wait and see.'

'We can't wait much longer,' I retorted. 'We've been waiting for something to happen for months.'

'Yes, I know, but don't worry about it. Create an atmosphere in which the Holy Spirit can work — a friendly, loving, even humorous atmosphere.'

'Yes,' I agreed. 'I'm not really worried. I don't mind if the Prayer and Praise Group ceases to exist as it is at the moment.'

'That's right. Stay calm. I'll pray for you.'

Good old Shena!

Off I went to Lorna's a few minutes later. She had been weighing up the tongues and interpretation at the last Tuesday meeting and had found a clue as to its meaning in her book.

'The sharp sword of the Spirit will pierce to the very centre of the group, but it will not cut or cause a wound.'

'Well,' I sighed, '*I* don't see how the sword can come in without a division.'

We decided that it would be useful to know what the others wanted in and from the meeting and after a brief exchange of ideas and encouragement I left to collect the children from school.

As I drove through the evening traffic, I thought, 'How *am* I going to handle this tonight? I'm sure I don't know the solution. I don't want to force people to pray or praise God when they don't have the inclination to. After all, God gives them free will, so what right has anyone else to compel. On the other hand, I am not willing to compromise my faith, to quench the Spirit or to disobey God's command to praise and take a closer walk with Him.'

I was still pondering later whilst cooking the dinner, when there was a knock on the door. It was Shena. She had brought me one of her poems, written before she became a Christian. It was so lovely, so calming that it brought peace to my mind. She had written:

Time always comes, my love;
Have not your fear.
Listen with care, my love,
To your inward ear.

Hark to the sound, my love;
Listen with care.
All that you wish to know
Is hidden there.

It was like a riddle. I knew that I had to listen, but for what?

Shena came to the meeting after all and I was very glad of her presence as she had a valuable contribution to make. After a prayer committing the evening to the Lord, I opened up the discussion with a comment about the rumoured dissatisfaction with the format. There was soon a lively flow of ideas underway with more openness than there had been for months. Many 'improvements' were suggested and I thanked the Lord for the restraint he gave me in not saying, 'But we've *tried* that to no avail!'

During a lull I asked if individuals could explain what they hoped to get out of the evening, and what they thought God wanted from it. The latter question was ignored. I let the chatter swirl around me, as though an on-looker, and let many remarks, which would usually have been like a red rag to a bull for me, pass by, hopefully to disintegrate of their own accord, rather like that same bull, which can hardly be roused on a sweltering summer afternoon, to flick even the most impertinent of flies with its tail.

As I listened it became clear to me that what several members of the group wanted was a 'Support Group', a refuge which would answer their needs for friendship, identification, encouragement, even occasionally for prayer for themselves or loved ones, a place to share these needs and be sure of being helped and understood. As I suggested this to them there was an almost audible sigh of relief and assent. We all agreed that this was an important part of being in the Christian family. We felt united at this point; we relaxed even further and there was a feeling of camaraderie.

However, I felt bound to point out that there may be some of us who also felt the need to come together at another time and place to praise God, come close to Him, listen to His voice and possibly act as a prophetic voice to the church. This was not contested and we ended with one hymn of praise.

As we piled into cars to go home, Shena said, 'Now you

will tell me when we're going to meet for prayer and praise, won't you. I can't do without that.' Another indicated likewise. The next morning I had a phone call from another member who had been absent, saying, 'I've heard that there is no Prayer and Praise now. But I need it! That's what I come for. If you arrange another time, I'll come to it!' That was greatly unexpected and encouraging.

I counted up and discovered that five people wanted a Praise Group, and five did not, exactly half and half. Then I realised, that the sword had pin-pointed the hub of the problem, the need for personal support, but the solution had not been divisive, in fact it had had a healing effect. As a bonus, there had also arisen a remnant, a nucleus for a new Praise Group, free from the old restrictions, urgently desiring to drink at the well of living water.

How well the Lord had engineered it all so far. There had been a split but not a rift. Now we had a new problem. How could we fit in another meeting into our busy week to suit everybody. I was sure the Lord had that one sorted out too, if we were only willing to wait on Him.

LISTEN — WAIT — TEACH

Chapter 14
A Prayer and Exhortation

August 1985

*'Now go and write down this word of mine…that
for the days to come it may be an everlasting
witness…For if you don't write it, they will claim I
never warned them, "Oh, no," they'll say, "you
never told us that!" For they are stubborn rebels.
They tell my prophets, "Shut up — we don't want
any more of your reports." Or they say, "Don't tell
us the truth, tell us nice things; tell us lies. Forget
all this gloom, we've heard more than enough
about your Holy One of Israel and all he says."'*

(Isaiah 30:8-11 LB, NIV)

O.K. Lord. I'll carry on writing — though I can't see
where it's leading. I sometimes wonder if I'm under a
delusion! Very little has changed. The barriers to renewal
have not been removed. We plod along from week to week,
praying and hoping —

*'Now faith is being sure of what we hope for and
certain of what we do not see.'* (Hebrews 11:1
NIV)

— but Lord — What are *you* doing? Lord, you are
stretching our faith and patience to the utmost. We would
have expected more growth after all this time. Even those
who have been baptised in the Spirit have not grown as they
should. How long can we continue in this desert,
under-nourished, and wandering blindly. It's all very well

150

gathering dew-drops, Lord, but we'll slowly die without solid food. The cactus flowers, though few and far between *are* beautiful, but they don't *feed* us, Lord.

Lord will you ever come and plant your shining cross on our hill? Will you come and keep your promise?

> *'The Lord still waits for you to come to him, so he can show you his love; he will conquer you to bless you just as he said. For the Lord is faithful to his promises. Blessed are all those who wait for him to help them.'* (Isaiah 30:18 LB)

Lord we have waited so long, and while we wait our young people are starving. Who can blame them for moving on to richer pastures? In times of famine, people travel miles to find food. Lord come quickly, or maybe, in a few months, more will have moved away. The people must be able to see that you answer prayer and keep your promises.

> *'Now turn from your sins! If you don't I will come to you soon and fight against those people with the sword that comes out of my mouth. If you have ears to hear, then, listen to what the Spirit says to the churches! To those who win the victory I will give some of the hidden manna.'* (Revelation 2:7 GNB)

But Lord we pray for more than a lonely flagstaff on top of the hill (Isaiah 30:17). We pray for you to come in mercy — to be our teacher — to show us your love and power — to turn us back to you in great numbers — in obedience and humility.

> *'Oh my people in Jerusalem, you shall weep no more for he will surely be gracious to you at the sound of your cry. He will answer you. Though he give you the bread of adversity and the water of affliction, yet he will be with you to teach you...And you will destroy all your idols...Then God will bless you with rain at planting time and with wonderful harvests and ample pasture...*
>
> *'In that day when God steps in to destroy your enemies he will give you streams of water flowing*

151

*down each mountain and every hill...When the
Lord begins to heal his people and cure the wounds
he gave them.'* (Isaiah 30:19-26 LB)

Thank you, Lord, for your strengthening and life-giving
word. Thank you for your encouragement as I remember the
signs you have given me that your hand is on this work. I
recall the strange dream that Jane had last October. She
telephoned me to ask if it had any significance.

*'There you were,' she said, 'carrying around a
huge empty barrel...(That was the unexpected
spare-time you had given me, Lord)...dithering,
wondering what to do with it. "How can I fill it
up?" you were wailing. Then suddenly, it was no
longer empty, but full of huge piles of paper with
writing on, manuscripts.'*

'Yes, Jane, I'm writing a book; please pray for me,' I
gasped, excitedly.

I had given up writing for several months, Lord,
discouraged by negative advice from a publishing
expert, and filled my time with busy-ness.

*'You ask advice from everyone but me, and decide
to do what I don't want you to do.'* (Isaiah 30:1 LB)

You brought me back to it in the autumn of '84 with that
sure word from Shena. You had sent her to her 'old' Bible,
and shown her Psalm 26:7 (KJV)

*'That I may **publish** with a voice of thanksgiving
and tell of all thy wondrous works.'*

Of course! The *wine-offering* (Psalm 116:13 GNB) *is* the
'hymn of thanksgiving' (Psalm 26:7 GNB), 'proclaiming
aloud your praise and telling of your wonderful deeds.'
(Psalm 26:7 NIV)

Lord, I want to be able to write of the most wonderful of
all your deeds — the fulfilling of a vision and the glory of
God in your church.

'And you will know the truth and the truth will set
you free. Know that my word will be written
through you to set you free in this situation. The

enemy has tried to trap you, but you are now free, free to be my instrument. You are to write in obedience as I have given you the words, and as I continue to give my wisdom in a spirit of prayer. And in my abiding presence, the truth which has set you free will be made known to others.'

('Dayspring': Anne White p.76)

Chapter 15
Possess the Land

January 1984 — July 1985

> *'Call unto me and I will show you great and mighty things which thou knowest not'*
>
> (Jeremiah 33:3 KJV)
>
> 'Pray as I tell you, even if you do not understand yet. It will come clear eventually. I will not leave you orphans. Follow my footprints through the snow, through the woods. Though you cannot see ahead the way is not unknown. It is a planned pathway. The snow indicates my purity and reflects my light. The footprints show where another has gone before. Your prints will show others where you've been.' (Lydia Book 26.9.83 5.12.83)

It was true that we did not always understand the prophecies the Lord gave us, especially in the matter of timing. Was it a forthtelling for today, or was it a foretelling of an event that would come to pass in the future?

Way back in October '83 we were given a picture of an army climbing up our hill and planting a flag on the summit. With it was an exhortation to 'possess the land'. How were we to do that? Was it totally metaphorical, or were we to obey literally in order to be blessed? It was all rather puzzling, but we held on to the promise in Isaiah 60:22 GNB:

> *'When the right time comes, I will make this happen quickly. I am the Lord'.*

As we swept into the much-heralded year of 1984 our

154

attention was taken up with the wider issues of Mission England, Mission to London, and the miners' strike. Bruce, Lorna and I attended a course for counsellors and were thrilled to participate in the rallies at the QPR football ground. To our delight, three from our house-groups and three of our teenagers went forward at Luis Palau's invitation and made a step of commitment to Jesus. The Lord had promised us in May:

'Pray for obedience in my people. Then I will reveal myself in a personal encounter'.

This diversion was a blessing, for I was beginning to feel lethargic about West Wycombe. I allowed my own house-group to fold up as I sensed we were entrenched in a no-growth situation. There were often only two or three of us in the Lydia meetings. I wondered how much longer I could 'stick it out'. It was Luis Palau who rapped me on the knuckles. During a rousing speech to launch the London campaign, he had thundered a warning:

'All those who are thinking of leaving their churches! I have one word for you — DON'T!'

I was going through a very dry time, personally. It worried me that my praying had become joyless and that the Bible was not 'coming alive' for me as it used to. This was probably due to the fact that I was harbouring resentments in my heart, though I did not realise the connection at the time.

God is so good. That summer he introduced Bruce and me to a lovely group of Christians who met in a neighbouring district on a Thursday night. They were all from different churches, but were drawn together by a common need for teaching and a time of closeness to the Lord in worship. There, I found I could relax in an atmosphere of acceptance and love, whilst being strengthened for the week ahead.

God soon began to work on me in that group. He pin-pointed the resentments I felt against my own husband regarding the way he worked such long hours. I recognised that I had prayed for him to enjoy his work in a flourishing company, but now regretted its implications. The Spirit began to open a way of true forgiveness.

I had allowed the devil to speak the voice of reason and deceit to me. He had convinced me that if I forgave Bruce, the situation would only worsen, because he would assume I did not mind being an office-widow. Through hearing a story about a Russian Christian who loved his torturers, I realised that love does not necessarily condone, and if the prisoner hates his jailer, it only harms the prisoner himself.

I must add that it was several months after I had confessed my unforgiveness that I was really able to let go of it, but what peace when I did. There was, of course, the extra bonus that my change of attitude enabled me to offer a warmer welcome for which to come home early.

Lorna knew that I needed encouragement. She gave me a verse from Isaiah 30 for my comfort:

> 'The Lord will make you go through the hard times,
> but he himself will be there to teach you, and you
> will not have to search for him any more. If you
> wander off the road to the right or the left you will
> hear his voice behind you saying "Here is the road.
> Follow it."'   (v20-21 GNB)

However, we both knew our enthusiasm was waning. The Lord continually exhorted us in Lydia meetings:

> 'Repent about complacency. Run with
> determination. Do not give up'   (4.4.84)
> 'Stick with it. Keep trusting. Remain in the
> Vine'.   (21.5.84)
> 'You *shall* reap if you faint not. The Lord *will*
> come and not be slow.'   (10.9.84)

In the first week of October I was bothered by a snatch of a song that would not leave me. It had first entered my head in Lorna's front room whilst I was asking the Lord how to pray:

> 'Your word is mighty — releasing captives'

During our prayer time we related this phrase to people we knew who were captive in their personal circumstances to tradition and fear of change; one was a Jew, one a Freemason, and one a clergyman.

I knew the words 'releasing captives' were very important. Whilst meditating in my own quiet time on the passage Lorna had given me in Isaiah 30, I read on as far as verse 25.

> *'On the day when the forts of your enemies are captured and their people are killed, streams of water will flow from every mountain and every hill.'*

I suspected that this was a key verse. On the following Lydia day I asked Lorna to prayerfully read the whole passage, from verse 19-26, and to tell me which verse she thought we ought to pray about. She confirmed my conviction about verse 25.

We knew we had to pray for the capture of enemy fortresses and the release of the captives from them. But what did this mean? We asked the Lord to show us what the fortresses were. He replied: the caves, the House, Hallowe'en (including the celebrations at the school), and the Church. Because of inadequate teaching and inhibition, the church is not effectively releasing those minds which have been captured by the devil, binding them in pre-conceived ideas and the outward forms of religion.

That one's mind is in bondage to the devil's deceits is not to be taken as a personal criticism or as a slur on one's character. The devil is constantly attempting to attack people's minds, especially those who would battle against him. Often we do not realise it until we have been set free, or until the Holy Spirit gives us discernment over it. If the devil has set my mind in a mould which pleases him because it hinders the growth of my relationship with God, then I am captive to him, and need to be released by the authority of Jesus being proclaimed to the enemy.

After much meditation, prayer and discussion, Lorna said, 'Hallowe'en is the traditional Samhain festival when occultists intensify their activities. We must engage in a counter-attack of prayer at the same time to neutralise their influence. I think we should ask other Christians to help us'.

After that we began a daily onslaught of prayer using the words of Isaiah 30:25 from various translations.

'Lord we pray for the capture of the enemy fortresses and strongholds in our midst, that the towers may fall (NIV), and that you would release the captives'. And from 2 Chronicles 20:33 we added, 'Destroy the high places of pagan worship, that the people may turn wholeheartedly to worshipping you!'

I shared our prayer-burden with the Thursday Fellowship and suggested some might be interested in joining us in spiritual warfare over Hallowe'en. One member remarked, 'There's an evil influence connected with the golden ball. It fell off once and now is chained on.'

Another prophesied, 'In my mind I see chains around West Wycombe that need to be cut'.

Over the following couple of weeks I was heartened to find that we had support coming from all sides of the town, from spiritually discerning Christians, some of whom saw West Wycombe as the key to revival for the whole area. I telephoned an old friend from St. Andrew's Lydia group to ask for her prayers. 'Oh', she exclaimed, 'we prayed for you, and West Wycombe, two days ago. Yes, we are behind you'.

The Lord showed us a picture of thorns surrounding our church and reminded us, from Numbers 33:55, that the Israelites were told to drive out the enemy from the Promised Land, or else they would become like thorns in their sides and fight against them. They were given no option; it was God's command, and if they did not obey, the Lord would allow them, his chosen people, to be destroyed. (v.56)

He also told us:

'Not by might or power, but by my Spirit, the obstacles will disappear. You need the weapons of

God to destroy the strongholds,'
(from Zechariah 4:6, 2 Corinthians 10:4 GNB)
and the whole armour of God for your protection'.

'Take possession, my children take up your
weapons and take possession.'   (Lydia 29.10.84)

On reflection we realised that there is only one weapon for
our use — the sword of the Spirit, which is the Word of God.
In order to use it, it must be proclaimed.

It was decided to hold a special prayer meeting on the
evening of 31st October (Hallowe'en) and also a preparation
meeting a couple of day before. We were really blessed by
the way outsiders were willing to come and support us at
both meetings.

There were eight of us on the Monday evening, Lorna and
I, joined by friends from the Thursday Fellowship. That
night we paved the way with prayer for the Wednesday
meeting. We filled the Church-Room with praise for the
name and power of Jesus, removed the corn-dollies,*¹ and
claimed the place for the Lord's work. We prayed that those
who planned mischief or evil for the area should be
restrained, confused and scattered by the Holy Spirit. We
also asked for specific instructions regarding our course of
action. God said to us:

*'...Go up on a high mountain and proclaim the
good news!...Speak out and do not be afraid...The
Sovereign Lord is coming to rule with power,
bringing with him the people he has
rescued.'*   (Isaiah 40:9-10 GNB)

We also felt that we had to claim the hill with wooden
crosses, and trace the boundary from Kitty's Lodge in the
east to the Gate-House in the west, including the George and
Dragon (rumoured haunted) and the caves-entrance on the
hill-side.

One of the group was given a warning picture of a
darkly-clad man, with a worried face, running away along

---

*¹   A pagan symbol.

the crest of the hill, but, without realising where he was heading, he ran slap into the devil's clutches. We felt it was a reminder not to run away from the battle, for in so doing, the devil wins, but to face up to it, resisting, so that the devil will flee (James 4:7).

*****

We were delighted to find that the number of representatives from our village was trebled for the Hallowe'en meeting. We gathered again in the ancient Church Room with ten friends from neighbouring churches. Again our praise resounded as we sought to assure Satan of Jesus' victory over all evil. We prayed for the confusion of the enemy and a lessening of his power. As a further stand against the devil, we confessed our sin and washed ourselves metaphorically in the cleansing blood of Jesus.

Singing gave way to silence, as we waited on the Lord for his directions. There was a spiritual battle already being waged as our minds were attacked with feelings of doubt, inadequacy, inferiority and indecision. A spirit of resistance to the Holy Spirit set in for a while, until overcome by a word of encouragement from one of the bolder Christians among us. A prophecy in tongues followed, with the interpretation given:

'The Lord says, "I am breaking the chains."'

One of us had a sensation of 'pushing—giving birth'. We felt God engaged in a mighty work amongst us.

I am sure that the period of tension and inward-looking that followed was a last-ditch attempt from the enemy to weaken our defences. For a while, we took our eyes off Jesus and some criticism and dissension tried to take a hold. Some of us felt we must climb up to the crown of the hill, planting the wooden crosses we had made and claiming the land for the Lord. Others thought that the Lord's work had already been done in the meeting. It was suggested that those who wanted to leave, for any reason, should do so, since it was already ten-thirty.

Six people left, some to return to husbands and children at home. Amongst those who remained, there was a renewed sense of unity. We prayed for assurance of the task ahead and knew, with conviction, that we were to wage war on the hill at midnight.

We began to be strongly attacked by fear, sensing the presence of evil 'out there'. We addressed the demon of fear and told it to go, in Jesus' name. We claimed the Lord's armour and the boldness and power of the Holy Spirit. I felt calmer now, and although I hated the thought of being out on the hill that night, I was able to control my fear. I knew I *had* to go; I knew that the Lord expected obedience and I would have no peace if I let Him down.

Two of the group decided to stay in the Room and pray for the rest of us. Of the eight who ventured forth, only two were from West Wycombe, and only one of those was from St. Lawrence's. It was shortly after 11.30 when we left the relative warmth and light of the Church Room and stepped out into the darkness, clutching our crosses. We walked purposefully up Church Lane and made our first stop at the triangle beyond the last house. A cross was planted and we huddled together in prayer.

As I turned from the glow of the windows and faced the close blackness of the hill road, I hardly dared wonder what to expect. Would we catch a glimpse of hooded figures slinking away across the grass? Or would *they* be spying on *us* from behind the hedges, breathing curses on us and sacrificing cats? Would I feel icy fingers across my cheek, or even a bat in my hair? I told myself I was becoming quietly hysterical. I put my best foot forward and made sure I kept close to the others.

I soon realised that there would be no theatrical effects after all, but what we actually discovered was, in a way, far worse. Cars were continually passing us on their way up the hill, as we trudged along. I glanced upwards towards the church on our left and was horrified to see fireworks being let off in the grave-yard. As we neared the top we realised that hordes had arrived before us and the noise of revelry was all around.

'It's crowded!' I gasped.

We pressed on, knowing we must reach the summit. We stopped as soon as the ridge was attained but dared not move any nearer the church. I recoiled, sickened by the spectacle. It seemed to be surrounded by alien groups, dressed in weird costumes with grotesque masks, screeching and shouting, many the worse for drink.

Most were there, I am sure, seeking a thrill from the evil associations of Hallowe'en. Many had come out of curiosity, drawn by the same fascination that persuades one to watch a horror movie. Some had even brought children for 'a night out'! Did they realise they were desecrating the temple? Did they set out to defy holiness? Probably not; it was merely the superficial out-working of a deeper evil that we had already experienced that night, in the Church Room.

We planted a cross at the highest point and took possession of the land for Jesus Christ! We claimed dominion in Jesus' name over the devil and all his works! We looked out over the valley towards High Wycombe and proclaimed Jesus' victory over all the land that we could see! As groups brushed past us on either side, I was scared. We gritted our teeth, prayed in tongues, and praised the Lord.

Since none of us had any inclination to approach the melée on the apron of the hill, we retraced our steps down the road, giving a holy shout and bore right, this time, past the caves entrance. One of our group walked straight up to the gates and said to a couple loitering there, 'Excuse me. I want to plant a cross.' They disappeared in a flash.

We continued to pray and leave crosses as we came round by the school, and then crossed the High Street to gather around the gates of Dashwood House. Here, we said the Lord's Prayer together.

'Our Father, who art in heaven,
Hallowed by thy name — here;
Thy kingdom come — here;
Thy will be done — here;
On earth as it is in heaven.
Give us this day our daily bread — here;
And forgive us — here — our trespasses as we forgive
them that trespass against us — here;
And lead us not into temptation — here;
But deliver us from evil — here;
For thine is the kingdom — here
the power — here
and the glory — here
For ever and ever — here
Amen.

It was a very moving experience.

We returned, prayerfully, past the George, and finally, Kitty's Lodge at the Pedestal. At that moment, I never wanted to go on such an adventure again, and yet I knew that, if God wanted me to, I would. I had sensed the power of God at work that night. It was exhilarating.

* * * * *

A friend who was praying for us that night at home, was given a picture in her mind of chains being pulled apart. The chains became ropes breaking, the strands of which became fingers letting go.

That week it was noticed that the light which illuminated the golden-ball, for the benefit of miles around, went out. A year later, it still had not been replaced.

Lorna invited me to report my experience to the Vicar and Parochial Church Council. Although I was accused by some of being alarmist over a 'bit of harmless fun', it was agreed to hold a service in the church in future years to deter unwelcome visitors. A request for a cross to be mounted on our church, as a sign of God's presence, was also agreed to. Praise the Lord!

* * * * *

Lorna and I knew that the work had only just begun. We prayed for more pray-ers and waited on the Lord for further instructions. He gave Lorna an inspiring prophecy:

> 'Weep not, nor faint, for the Lord is with you. Remember Mary Magdalene who anointed my feet.[2] Raise your arms in prayer, ask and it will be given you. Strengthen yourselves for the time ahead. There will be tribulation but with courage and strength you will win through. The axe is laid at the root of the tree of evil. Strengthen yourselves in prayer, Lift me up, and I will raise you. My children, you are gold and I will refine you.
> Listen and I will speak;
> Touch and I will heal.
> Let the nations praise my holy name.'

By December, we knew that the next prayer battle would take place near Christmas. God told us to arrange a special meeting in the Church, beginning in the chancel, and moving out as directed. We were to meet at 8.00 a.m. on the Saturday before Christmas Day and to take the remainder of the wooden crosses with us. We prayed that there would be a greater number of pray-ers from West Wycombe than from the other churches this time.

[2]   Luke 7:47

The sun shone early that Saturday morning and in spite of the urgency of Christmas shopping, eight members of our congregation had responded to our invitation to meet in St. Lawrence's, and we were joined by four faithful supporters. We placed a cross in the middle of our circle of chairs and read:

> *'Arise, Jerusalem, and shine like the sun. The glory of the Lord is shining on you!'*   (Isaiah 60:1 GNB)

For the next couple of hours we praised the name and glory of Jesus and prayed for the cleansing and rededication of our church and grounds. We were given a picture of a protecting wall being built outside the door of the church. The interpretation is also to be found in Isaiah 60, verse 18 GNB:

> *'The sounds of violence will be heard no more. Destruction will not shatter your country again. I will protect and defend you like a wall; You will praise me because I have saved you.'*

On our way outside, we stopped by the font and marble sun set in the floor of the nave, and claimed them for the glory of God, releasing them from any idolatrous connotations. Once in the churchyard, we proclaimed the Lordship of Jesus over the grounds and mausoleum. We prayed for the protection of the entrances and in our minds' eye drew a line of blood around the boundary.

As we stood on the eastern edge overlooking Wycombe, I was conscious of the fact that the caves were directly beneath me, three hundred feet down, and prayed that any evil they might hold would be flushed out. It was a heady reminder that in the heavenly order, we are raised with Christ, high above the devil and his minions.

Later, we heard that a family decorating the Christmas tree in the church that afternoon had said with amazement, 'We really felt the presence of God here today!'

* * * * *

For a few months there was a waiting time. I felt the frustration of being cut off from the Lydia Group whilst I worked at the school as a supply teacher for two terms. However, the Lord faithfully brought two or three together to pray at a constant rate of once a month. I was told that they were praying for the Word of God to be preached with authority and power from the church. Lorna and I resumed our practice of meeting together as prayer partners, in the church, early on Saturday mornings.

'*I* don't think we *will* have a cross on our church until the Word of God is preached there,' confided Lorna.

Prophecy bites hard when we don't like the message, but it was a fact that nothing had been undertaken regarding that P.C.C. decision on the cross, eight months earlier. This, however, did not deter us from praying for its coming reality and the fulfilment of the vision.

We became aware of others in our church who felt uncomfortable about the golden ball, and wished for the symbol of truth to replace it. Whilst escorting tourists up the tower one Saturday afternoon, Bruce remarked that he would like to see the ball removed.

'Oh, you can't do that', remonstrated the visitor. 'It's the symbol of all that is evil around here, isn't it!'

Well, you cannot have both symbols vying for pride of place. Our great and mighty God is Lord over all. He is a jealous God.

> '*For thou shalt worship no other God*'
>
> (Exodus 34:14 RSV)
>
> verse 11 *"So be very careful to love the Lord your God. 12 But if you turn away and allay yourselves with the survivors of these nations that remain among you'...*(NIV)
>
> verse 13 *'they will be as dangerous for you as a trap and as painful as thorns in your eyes. And this will last until none of you are left on this good land which the Lord has given you.' (GNB)*
>
> (Joshua 23:11-13)

Taking our eyes off Jesus, and looking down at the facts surrounding us, we felt despondent that there were no visible results from our prayer attack before Christmas. There was no evidence of change either in our sevices or in personal commitment, and the house-groups appeared to be marking-
time in the same old mould of resistance and compromise. No one had emerged with a calling to join the work of prayer, of evangelism or teaching.

What a blessing then to hear from a friend that in other areas of Wycombe a spirit of openness and release was being experienced and it was regarded as a result of the releasing prayer from West Wycombe.

Of the four strongholds of the enemy, two had been dealt with — Hallowe'en and the Church, though we continued to pray for people who were prisoners to tradition. A lovely Jewish lady who had been greatly influenced by Diana, began coming to services, and shortly after we had begun to pray for her release, she decided to be baptised. On the other hand, the Freemason we had prayed for decided to leave our church.

I avoided the question of the Caves, since Dom Robert had assured us that they were dealt with, and we had recently prayed above them and at the gates. And anyway, the idea of actually entering them revolted me.

We turned our attention, therefore, to the Dashwood Estate and asked the Lord for further directions. We were concerned by the fact that the grounds had once been designed as a shrine to immorality, intended as a rebellion against purity and godliness.

'For rebellion is as bad as the sin of witchcraft.'
(1 Samuel 15:23 NIV)

Sir Francis was an expert in Classical Art, which being pre-Christian was of course Pagan. The characteristics of paganism — idolatry and immorality — were to be publically seen in the Park until about 1794 when Repton, a landscapist, was hired to make judicious alterations. The suggestive layout of flower beds was put to lawns, and erotic statuary removed. However, the numerous follies remained as temples to the gods.

The west portico of the House is a copy of the Temple of Bacchus (the Greek god of wine) and is said to have been the first attempt in England to incorporate Greek architecture into an English manor house. It was opened ceremonially with a three-day pagan festival and grand pageant. Drunken revellers, dressed as priests and priestesses, fauns and satyrs, sang the praises of Bacchus.

The Temple of Venus was built in 1748, just prior to the harvest failures, and coinciding with the founding of the Hell Fire Club. Recently in 1982 this temple was restored, the work being hailed as a triumph with more celebrations. The spirit of paganism was still covering that land.

We knew what we must do. I met Lorna at the Park gates after school, one afternoon in July. Having bought our tickets we proceeded to walk the grounds beginning with the path that lies parallel to the High Street and River Wye. We paused on a little bridge over a stream that entered the Park from under the road.

'Could this be the River Styx?' we wondered. It was quite possible that that river, said to arise at the Inner Temple in the depths of the caves, permeated through the chalk hill and issued as springs under the High Street, which in turn were piped into the Wye at this point. No matter whether our geography was correct — this was the place at which we *must* pray first.

Praise the Lord! We had the park almost to ourselves. I must admit feeling a little self-conscious, praying so publically for the murky black waters to become white. Was this what St. Paul meant by 'fools for Christ' (1 Corinthians 4:10)? After a few minutes the peace of the Holy Spirit overcame me and I sensed the importance of our assignment.

Following the track over the river, we arrived at the Temple of Venus, perched on a small mound. We climbed to the top and claimed the site for the Lord's purpose, praying for its cleansing from all past sin and repenting of the fact that we shared the guilt as inhabitants of West Wycombe.

Under the mound was a stone alcove, large enough to step into. It was more spacious than expected, and though we had no idea of its function, we *had* to pray there. I shall never forget the look on a certain tourist's face when he peered into the cave, only to find two women, one standing guard over the entrance, and the other talking to herself as she paced the perimeter.

Our crusade took us across the lake, out to the eastern boundary where the Wye makes for open country, and then north to the Temple of the Four Winds. This was a foreboding place, dank and dark. We claimed the Lordship of Jesus over it and moved on nearer to the Mansion, claiming the Dovecott Temple, Apollo Arch and finally the Temples of Bacchus and Flora.

We felt no need to enter the House, and later discovered why. The Lord had appointed that task to a clergyman from a neighbouring district who had moved from room to room during his visit consecrating each with holy water. We were delighted to hear, also, that he had been prompted to throw a cross into the lake!

It is lovely, the way the Lord confirms what we feel in our hearts by giving the same instructions to other people. When I received a Lydia prayer and news letter for the Bucks Area, stating that the leadership had received the command to possess the 'high hills of the Chilterns', I could have danced for joy.

The letter read, 'We have decided to 'tread upon' the whole scarp slope of the Chiltern Hills in Buckinghamshire, beginning at Ivinghoe's Beacon Hill and ending at Chinnor Hill. We have divided the area up into sections and arranged ourselves into groups, each with a co-ordinator. We are asking each group to possess their part of the land by September'.

We were reminded that to 'tread' means to crush or trample:

'You shall tread down the wicked'

(Malachi 4:3 RSV)

'Every place that the sole of your foot will tread upon, I have given to you…'   (Joshua 1:3 GNB)

Of course, Lorna and I agreed to join with other Lydia's in the area, and spent a memorable morning in the pouring rain, treading the high places from St. Lawrence's to Bledlow Ridge Church, a small link in a chain of praying, praising, women marching for the Lord.

Chapter 16
The Key — A New Vision

October 1985

'Right! Let's get out of here as quickly as we can. I never want to visit this place again. I wouldn't be at all surprised if the whole system collapses now'. We hurried to the exit of West Wycombe Caves. It was evident, where the occasional lamp beamed its dim light, that damp mist was gathering around us. If only I had brought my torch. The Lord had provided the rest of our equipment — the bowls, the salt, the words.

We had been given an instruction from 2 Kings 2, to go and sprinkle salt into the springs, to make the water pure and wholesome.

> *The men of the city said to Elisha, "Look, our Lord, this town is well situated, as you can see, but the water is bad and the land is unproductive."*
>
> *"Bring me a new bowl," he said, "and put salt into it." So they brought it to him.*
>
> *Then he went out to the spring and threw the salt into it'.*   (v.19-21a NIV)

We knew we had to go to the source of the River Styx, so named in 'Hell-Fire days' because of its associations with Hades. The spring originally arose in the 'Cursing Well' deep in the caves, and the stream passed in front of the cavern known as the Inner Temple. Not so long ago, a boat was needed in order to cross it, but since the water-table has lowered, the stream has been reduced to a mere trickle and requires a pump to keep the level up, as a tourist attraction.

However, it has been been proved by pot-holers that the Styx still flows, or rather seeps, away from the caves, though it is not known exactly where it reappears. It is probably part of the same river system as the Wye which arises behind the Garden Centre at the end of the village, and flows under the main road, through the Dashwood estate, and on past Wycombe to feed the Thames.

I had still been reluctant to enter the caves, but after much prayer had decided with Lorna to undertake in faith the task of salting this spring, and also the more geographical source of the Wye. Praise the Lord for our Indian summer, for the Estate Office had kept the caves open till the end of October. Now in the last week of the season, we were the only two visitors.

On arriving in the heart of the caves we had poured salt into new pottery bowls and prayed for the Lord's work to be done. Our prayer coincided ominously with a peal of bells from the tape that was playing. 'You are now 300ft deep at the site of the River Styx', it had declared. We had thrown the salt into the water and proclaimed the words from Scripture.

'This is what the Lord says: "I have healed this water. Never again will it cause death or make the land unproductive".'   (2 Kings 2:21 NIV)

Just as we completed our task, the bells chimed again.

Dom Robert had once assured us that these caves had often been exorcized, but, hurrying through the gloom now, it was difficult to believe. I did not normally have a fear of caves, but I definitely sensed God's judgement upon this place.

What a relief to emerge outside again, blinking in the daylight, though it was a dull day, threatening rain. As we made our way down to the field, there was time to consider the way that water had often featured in the pictures the Lord had given us. He had promised:

172

'The waters will not overcome you'

(Lydia 10.1.83)

'When my people in their need look for water...then I, the Lord will answer their prayer...I will make rivers flow among barren hills and springs of water run in the valleys. I will turn the desert into pools of water and the dry land into flowing springs'.   (Isaiah 41:17-1 GNB)

(Lydia 7.3.83)

Way back in January '83, the Lord had referred us to Ezekiel 47 — the stream flowing from the Temple. This is such a well known passage that one tends to read it with a closed mind, as I did at first, merely appreciating that the Water of Life comes from Jesus who refreshes our lives when we let him flow through us. 'How lovely', I thought, 'if the Water of Life were to flow through West Wycombe'.

However, the Lord set to work on my blindness, till I began to see an amazing similarity with the river said to arise in the caves. In Ezekiel 47:2, the prophet is taken to the eastern gate of the Temple where a small stream flowed at the south side. Last Christmas our little band of pray-ers went out of the church and stood at the eastern gate — the original entrance to St. Lawrence's churchyard. I had moved a few paces to the south of this gate (note v.2) and as I stood there on the hill top, I had sensed the source of the River Styx below me in the caves. As I had prayed there for the cleansing of the stream, I never expected to be sent on such a mission as we were now engaged upon.

Wherever Ezekiel's stream flowed, there was the promise of new life (v.9) and of fruitfulness (v.12). The trees that were watered by this river would provide food and healing for the people. (v.12)

Those who follow occult or idolatrous practices, seek the reversal of those things pertaining to God. Thus those who had pursued evil in our local history had also recognised the picture of the stream issuing from the temple; indeed had named the river, flowing from the 'Inner Temple', to glorify

173

Hades. Since then there had been no fruitfulness, no feeding, no healing, no productiveness.

In Ezekiel's vision, the river flowed eastward to the sea, where it caused the salt water to become fresh. (v.8) Now, God was telling us to use *salt* to freshen the water. How can salt make water fresh and clean? I believe the answer is to be found in Numbers 21:9.

When the people of Israel complained against God in the wilderness, poisonous snakes were sent among them to bite them, as a punishment. The Israelites repented of their sin and pleaded with Moses to persuade God to remove the plague. God decreed that they were to mount a bronze snake on a pole, and were to look at the God-given snake in order to be healed of the effect of the harmful snakes.

Jesus used this example in John 3:14 to show that the world was to look to the God-sent Man in order to be healed of the consequences of sinful man. In West Wycombe the Lord has used God-given salt to heal water polluted by sin.

As we stood at the source of the River Wye, I was conscious of the fulfilment of a prophecy given last year.

'There will be a river of life flowing through the
village and you will help people to drink from it.';
'I will be your shepherd'　　　　Micah 7:14 GNB)

Emptying the salt into the spring, we prayed that it would be carried along on the current, cleansing all on its course from the guilt and stigma of the past. What excitement as we realised there was now the potential for our land to be productive and fruitful. It is surely no coincidence that the Wye is a tributary of the Thames. That great river, on whose banks stand the Houses of Parliament, our seat of government, flows through the centre of our capital city. Waters once cursed by a parliamentary cult in West Wycombe caves, now have been symbolically purified.

*****

That same evening five Christians met in our living room on urgent prayer-business. We were thrilled that this year, for the first time, the vicar had arranged to hold a communion service in St. Lawrence's on the Eve of All Saints Day, or Hallowe'en. He had announced that the service, to be held at ten o'clock at night, was intended to be a witness in the face of evil. By heavenly planning Thursday nights are also for choir and bell-ringing practice! What an opportunity to ring out the praises of the Lord.

Lorna and I felt that this year needed no less preparation than last. We enlisted the support of the Thursday Fellowship again, and set to, making a straight road for the Holy Spirit to move in. With heart-felt praise, we raised the throne of Jesus in our midst, and paved the way with prayer for the success of the All Saints Service. We prayed that it really would be a witness to all, of the Lord's presence on the hill. We prayed for the fulfilling of a prophecy that 'the glory of the Lord would fill the house'. What a joy as the Lord spoke words of inspiration to us:

'Proclaim my word. I am coming in power with healing in my wings'.

As a result of a suggestion at this meeting, Lorna and I visited the churchyard on Thursday afternoon. In Jesus' name, we placed an angel at each corner of the church building, and claimed the protection of the Lord's angels at the entrances too. We prayed that these angels might be equipped with sharp swords to keep at bay the agents of darkness. We declared that the devil had no right to trespass within these gates, and would be banished. The stage was set.

* * * * *

Praise the Lord, the creator of rain, that there was a fine drizzle early on Thursday evening — just enough to make

175

one think twice about a night out in the open-air. Bruce and I set off as usual for the Fellowship and were delighted to find that many of our friends there were planning to accompany us to the service later. Between spiritual songs of praise, we prayed that the bells would ring out from West Wycombe that night with a two-fold purpose: first to summon all Christians to come out and be witnesses on the Lord's side, and secondly to deter those who might venture forth from the enemy's ranks.

On entering the church a couple of hours later, I felt a quickening in my spirit that this would be a night to remember. The church was already almost full and I was overjoyed to see pews filled not only with St. Lawrence members, but also elders and friends from other parts of the Wycombe district. 'Nations will be drawn to your light and kings to the dawning of your new day' (Isaiah 60:3).*¹

The church was warm, and smiling faces beamed in recognition of one another across the nave. I sensed a special atmosphere of love that I had never before noticed here and a peace in my heart.

The service was beautiful. Never before had I known such a vibrant presence of the Holy Spirit in St. Lawrence's. For the first time in my experience, the liturgy, read with heaviness for so many Sundays previously, came into its own and had life. It reigned over the proceedings and proclaimed the Word of God. In the words of the 'Gloria' we sang:

> 'Glory to God in the Highest, and peace to his
> people on earth…We praise you for your Glory…
> Lamb of God who takes away the sin of the world
> Have mercy on us…You alone are the Lord, Jesus
> Christ with the Holy Spirit, In the glory of God the
> Father'.

---

*¹ Prophecy given in 1982.

The collect spoke of 'God's elect being knit together in one communion and fellowship, enjoying unspeakable joys'. Together we declared our faith in triumph in the words of the Creed, made righteous in the blood of Jesus through the Confession.

I am sure the choice of readings, from a selection laid down for All Saints' Day, must have been inspired by the Holy Spirit. Jeremiah 31 proclaimed:

> *'I will make a new covenant with Israel...I will become their God, and they shall become my people...I will forgive their wrong doing and remember their sin no more'.*

Lorna was asked to read the New Testament passage from Revelation 5. She announced:

> *'Salvation belongs to our God who sits upon the throne, and to the Lamb, For the Lamb in the midst of the throne will be their shepherd and he will guide them to springs of living water!'*

We stood to hear the vicar read the gospel. In the Beatitudes, the words of Jesus assured us:

> *How blest are those who hunger and thirst to see right prevail.*
> *They shall be satisfied...*

As we moved into the Communion, there was a strong witness of unity as we let down our barriers of reticence and actually 'passed the Peace'. As the Body of Christ we broke bread together across denominational divides and enjoyed being 'family'.

We poured our hearts out in the last hymn — 'For all the saints' — and remembered that those who had sown and those who reap rejoice together. As if this were not climax enough, the Post Communion Sentence declared:

> *'I heard the noise of a great multitude crying Allelujah! The Lord our God has entered into his Kingdom. Happy are those who are called to the supper of the Lamb.'*

It was eleven o'clock. All seemed quiet outside on the hill

as many drifted away home, a new love and excitement filling their hearts. Indeed some were even seen hugging one another.

About sixteen of us felt the need to continue the watch till midnight. Representatives from several different churches gathered at the back of the church to continue praising, using the powerful scriptural words of the new spiritual songs. In word and music we held the standard firm for Jesus for a further hour. After a while a commotion was heard outside the main door. Someone went out, praying loudly in tongues. The trespassers disappeared like vapour. We stepped up our praising, called upon the Lord's victory and declared that the powers of evil were banished.

A little later, I was alarmed to see, where the inner door was ajar, a group of people enter the porch. They approached the door and pushed it open. Those of us who saw them increased the volume of praising. 'We exalt Thee, we exalt Thee, O Lord!' The unwelcome visitors stepped one pace into the nave. I felt threatened. They were dressed in black, with a dark, dead look in their eyes, yet at the same time, menacing. We stood firm, praying and praising all the while, loudly and exultantly. After a few minutes they left. Several months previously, the Lord had said, 'My power will fill the church and break out through the door'. Now I understood.

As midnight drew near, I thought to myself, 'It's all very well feeling safe here in the church, but what's going on outside? We'll have to walk out to the car soon. We had better all keep close together. It won't be pleasant.' We walked as a group towards the north-gate. 'It's very quiet', I ventured to remark, hardly daring to believe it.

Once out on the open hill-top, the whole truth was clear. The hill was deserted. 'There's nobody here. There's *nobody here*!' We laughed with amazement as the glorious truth dawned on us. God *had* triumphed over evil, a victory had been won. Emotion swept over me and I felt weak at the knees. That night we had experienced the fulfilling of the vision. The radiance of the cross-victorious had shone from the church on the hill. Though symbolic, its effect was real. The light from the church windows had shone out in the darkness; the Light of the World had been proclaimed over West Wycombe. Those seeking evil had turned and fled away.

> *'they will come from their fortresses, trembling and
> afraid'*   (Micah 7:17) (Lydia 1.10.84)

The cross — the symbol of light, love, life, truth and the Word — had shone for all to see. Our prophecy from Isaiah 60 had said:

> *'But on you the light of the Lord will shine... You
> will see this and be filled with joy; you will tremble
> with excitement'.*

A PCC member who a year ago had been sceptical flung his arm around my shoulders and cried, 'It was worth it! You've taken a lot of flak — but it was worth it!'

* * * * *

'This is the *key*! This *is* the key!' A friend from our neighbouring parish had danced with joy as he announced these words after the gathering on Hallowe'en night. For years he had prayed for the release of the Holy Spirit in his own area. He had been given the wisdom and discernment to realise that West Wycombe had an influence over the surrounding district, that it was damming up the waters of spiritual life and preventing them from gushing down the valley into Wycombe. Now, in prophetic mood he could see that the hold of past circumstances, past sin and guilt had been removed and healed, and that the key, which had been stuck in the lock, has now been freed and turned, allowing that refreshing water, with all its power, to flow through.

West Wycombe *is* the key and is of vital importance to the town of High Wycombe. A key-stone is the central principal on which all depends. The key move in a game of chess is the first move a player makes. Now, the key piece of the jigsaw puzzle has been cleansed, freed and claimed, giving access for the Holy Spirit to move forward. The way to revival in Wycombe has been opened.

> 'Behold, I stand at the door and knock, if anyone
> hears my voice and opens the door, I will come in to
> him and eat with him.'   (Revelation 3:20 RSV)

Yes, the door to Wycombe has been opened, but whether or not renewal comes to West Wycombe itself depends on certain vital factors. It is of no use white-washing the past and pretending it never was as bad as its reputation. There is no good in brushing aside the wickedness and declaring it never was a sin at all.

> For 'arrogance (is) like the evil of idolatry'
>   (1 Samuel 15:23 NIV)

For self-justification never leads to the repentance which the Lord God Almighty requires of us in order for his blessings to flow. The land here has been cleansed and claimed for the Lord. There is the potential for the Holy Spirit to come in power and do great things among us, but this depends on the heart attitude of the people, and first of all, of the church.

God requires a personal turning back to Him, away from modern-day idolatry, especially the god of mammon. In whose pay are you? On whose money do you depend for your life? Are you dependent on a money-making venture (rather than evangelism and growth?) for the survival of your Church. Did Jesus endue the first Christians with the power of the Holy Spirit in order that they might start a 'Jumble Sale Church', or even, a tourist industry?

> 'Rebellion against him is as bad as witchcraft and
> arrogance is as sinful as idolatry. Because you
> rejected the Lord's command he has rejected you as
> King.'   (1 Samuel 15:23 GNB)

In this verse from Samuel, God shows us how seriously he views these sins in the removal of his blessing of Kingship from Saul. By God's grace we have been exonerated from the oppressive weight of accumulated evil from the past; the captives have been set free. We must not allow ourselves to be re-captured by the sins of the present. The Cross is the sign of freedom bought for us by Jesus Christ. We are not bound to sin any more, neither are we bound to set patterns or habits, nor to the rut of apathy, nor to sitting on the fence. There *is* another way. It needs an act of our will to follow it.

> 'Lift me up and reveal my glory. When I am lifted
> up I will draw all men to me. You will be
> free.'   (Lydia 9.9.85)

The Lord is calling his people to a deeper personal commitment to himself, putting him first in our lives, thirsting after a closer relationship with him. It involves a dying to 'self', a putting to death of our selfish desires and ambitions, before there can be any blossoming. It may also involve being 'a fool for Christ'. We need to have a love of his Word, to receive it as truth, not to argue against it or to compromise, but to accept it in obedience.

Picture an hour-glass, with the sands of time running out. Huddled in the top of the glass are the people who have turned to God, being held from falling through the hole by a pair of protecting hands, God's hands. (A picture given to Lorna's ladies' group.) Because he loves us so much, God wants to wonderfully bless those who will turn to him. We must admit our own weaknesses and sinfulness, acknowledge our need for salvation through Jesus Christ, and be willing to embrace the Holy Spirit, whose power will transform our lives and worship. He urges us:

> *'I am now giving you the choice between life and*
> *death, between God's blessing and God's curse,*
> *and I call heaven and earth to witness the choice*
> *you make. Choose life!'*

>   (Deuteronomy 30:16-20 GNB)

God is calling all to repentance, from the humblest villager to the highest rank, and he has given us a hope.

> *'Arise Jerusalem and shine like the sun. The glory*
> *of the Lord is shining on you! Nations will be drawn*

*to your light, and Kings to the dawning of your new
day'* (Isaiah 60:3 GNB)

'New people will kneel at your Communion rail
and drink deeply of the living water flowing out of
Jesus' side. Their roots will be nourished.'

(Lydia 21.2.83)

We now have a duty to keep the gateway to Wycombe
cleansed by prayer from further occult activity. Who will
accept the challenge to a deeper prayer-life, a closer walk
with God? Who will take on the responsibility of faith-full
praying, giving of precious time to wait on the Lord and
listen to his leading? The answer from everyone who calls
himself a Christian must be 'Here I am, Lord — send me.'[*2]

Looking out from West Wycombe Hill, on a clear day,
one can see for miles. The rolling countryside, crowned
with beechwoods, stretches away on every side, cradling to
the east, the town of High Wycombe in the valley of the
Wye. The scene that God created is beautiful, but it is not for
nothing that the devil is known as 'the prince of this world!'
Sites of heathen worship and occult practices abound, right
across the country. The Lord is grieving over these
fortresses where an intruder has staked his claim.

The Lord calls his church to look out from its watch-
towers and recognise the situation with Holy Spirit
discernment. He exhorts Christians everywhere to take up
this urgent work of cleansing and possessing the remainder
of the land, pushing out the frontiers for the Lord. Clear the
way of stones, prepare the ground for revival, for the Lord
is coming in power with healing in his wings.

Now is the time to come out from our prayer-cells and
claim this nation in Jesus' name. Tread the land which has
been under the ownership of those engaged in occult or
pagan habits. Trample the land polluted by witchcraft, past
or present, which is still tainted by immorality and the
blood-guilt of sacrifices. We have a commission to resist its

[*2] (Isaiah 6:8 KJV)

influence. Repent of inherited guilt and pray for the removal of the curse from the land.

We are called to march out like a victorious army, proclaiming the Lordship of Jesus over the nation. The time has come for praising him in a victory procession.

> *'I have given you, and all my people, the entire land that you will be marching over...Be determined and confident! Don't be afraid or discouraged, for I, the Lord your God, am with you, wherever you go.'* (Joshua 1:3,9)

It is important to wait on the Lord for specific instructions. Ask the Lord to identify the strongholds of darkness in your area, and then pronounce His victory over them, using His Word as the sword of the Spirit. It is time to speak out God's Word, both in prophetic prayer, and for an authoritative attack in spiritual warfare.

It may seem as though we pray in code, when we do not fully understand the Word, but if it is God-given, we need not be anxious. We do not need to understand the mechanism of a rifle before we can shoot on target. We only need to recognise the Shepherd's voice and obey it in faith. The Lord will honour this obedience.

Make a stand for Jesus — be an army — but also, shine like a cross on a hill. Our Holy God loves us and wants to bless us, but He is calling us to holiness too. How holy is the church? Are we keeping skeletons in our cupboards? Are there taboo subjects which must never be mentioned, no-go areas, vaults that must never be disturbed? Trample the devil, and his lies, underfoot; cast away barriers of fear, pride and apathy! Perfect love casts out fear. Do we hide our indiscretions under the carpet? Do we have secrets, guilty or otherwise, which are afraid of the light?

The Lord wants to shine *His* light into His church, and through them into the nation. Do not be a lamp that is hidden. Do not be a head-lamp that is dimmed by dirty glass. If the church is willing to shine in the darkness, the darkness will not be able to put it out!

The Lord says:

  I have anointed you,

  And my hand is upon you.

  The time of singing has come.

  The open fields stretch before you.

take my hand and walk out into the sunshine, my children,

My Spirit is with you and my blessings will abound.

My treasury is unlocked and my jewels pour forth in abundance.   (Lydia 21.11.85)

'Do not cling to events of the past or dwell on what happened long ago. Watch for the new thing I am going to do. It is happening already — you can see it now! I will make a road through the wilderness and give you streams of water there.'

      (Isaiah 43:18,19 GNB)

'Now unto Him that is able to do immeasurably more than all we ask or imagine, according to His power that is at work in us, to Him be the glory in the church and in Christ Jesus, throughout all generations for ever and ever. Amen.'

      (Ephesians 3:20,21 KJV)